Landscapes of
MALLORCA

a countryside guide
Sixth edition

Valerie Crespí-Green

SUNFLOWER BOOKS

Sixth edition © 2006
Sunflower Books™
PO Box 36160
London SW7 3WS, UK
www.sunflowerbooks.co.uk

Published in the USA by
Hunter Publishing Inc
130 Campus Drive
Edison, NJ 08818
www.hunterpublishing.com

ISBN 1-85691-306-6

Centuries-old olive tree below Lluc

Important note to the reader

We have tried to ensure that the descriptions and maps in this book are error-free at press date. The book will be updated, where necessary, whenever future printings permit. It will be very helpful for us to receive your comments (sent in care of the publishers, please) for the updating of future printings.

We also rely on those who use this book — especially walkers — to take along a good supply of common sense when they explore. Conditions can change fairly rapidly on Mallorca, and *storm damage or bulldozing may make a route unsafe at any time*. In November 2001 the worst winds ever recorded in the Balearics felled over 100,000 trees. Although the 'classic' routes should be cleared fairly quickly, it will take a long time to restore *all* the paths described in this book. If the route is not as we outline it here, and your way ahead is not secure, return to the point of departure. *Never attempt to complete a tour or walk under hazardous conditions!* Please read carefully the notes on pages 43 to 49, as well as the introductory comments at the beginning of each tour and walk (regarding road conditions, equipment, grade, distances and time, etc). Explore *safely*, while at the same time respecting the beauty of the countryside.

Cover photograph: Port d'Andratx
Title page: old well at Valldemossa

Photographs: pages 6, 12, 27 (bottom), 41 (bottom), 50, 52 (right), 53, 57 (middle), 61 (top), 63, 68, 72-73, 74-75, 76, 81, 83, 91 (all), 98 (top), 104, 109, 111, 113, 119, 125, 128 (bottom): Valerie Crespí-Green; 27 (bottom left), 52 (left), 94, 120, 121: Lawrence Crawley; 130: Joaquín Ranero Gascon; cover: i-stockphoto; all others: John Underwood
Maps: John Underwood
A CIP catalogue record for this book is available from the British Library.
Printed and bound in England by J H Haynes & Co Ltd

10 9 8 7 6 5 4 3 2 1

Contents

4   Landscapes of Mallorca

● Preface

When you think of Mallorca, do you imagine a typical holiday island — hotels and souvenir shops strung out along busy esplanades … bars advertising 'English Fish and Chips' and 'Tea Like Mum Makes' … a multitude of night clubs and discos with large and gaudy posters promoting flamenco shows? Do you think this is Mallorca? I hope not.

Of course, the hotel-crowded esplanades *do* exist, but beyond the tourist centres, an exciting and altogether different Mallorca awaits your discovery. And with this Sixth edition of *Landscapes of Mallorca,* I hope to help you to find it.

The book is divided into three main parts — **picnicking**, **touring** and **walking**, each with its own introduction. Do look over each introductory section, even if you think it may not apply to your holiday plans. You may find something of interest, because each section of the book has been written with one aim in view — to help you discover the 'hidden' Mallorca that many tourists never see.

Motorists will find that the six car tours cover more than enough territory for the average visit. The touring map has purposely been kept to a compact, easy-to-use format and contains information not found on many other maps, for instance the location of petrol stations and isolated restaurants, picnic sites with tables, and walks along the route of your car tour.

Picnickers can travel by private or public transport to all the picnic spots — some of them chosen for their delightful surroundings, others for their far-reaching views. All of the picnic suggestions make excellent 'leg-stretchers' during the course of a car tour, when there's no time to fit in a longer walk.

Walkers of all ages and abilities will enjoy discovering the island's hidden landscapes, as they cross an incredible variety of terrain — some spectacular, some serene. For beginners, there are easy strolls along flat tracks (for instance, Short walk 20, and others (like Walk 8 or Short walk 24) on delightful country lanes. Hardy walkers can tackle more challenging terrain to *miradors* that are only accessible on foot, and experts can scale mountain peaks or descend into the depths of the Pareis gorge …

Acknowledgements

I am extremely grateful for the invaluable help of the following:

For guiding: Mauricio Espinar, without whose knowledge and experience I could not have written the first edition of this book.

For permission to adapt their maps: The Servicio Geográfico del Ejército, Madrid.

For checking the walks and accompanying me: Clive Scott, the late George Clarke, Mary Clarke, Elizabeth and Klaus Pffeifer, Ann White, and Karen Roberts.

Cala S'Almonia (Car tour 5)

Getting about

There is no doubt that a **hired car** is the most convenient way of getting about on Mallorca, and car rental on the island is good value. Be sure to 'shop around' amongst the many car-hire firms (where English is generally spoken); the prices can vary by up to as much as 40 per cent!

The second most flexible form of transport is to hire a **taxi** and, especially if three or four people are sharing the cost, this becomes an attractive idea. If you're making a taxi journey outside the city centre (an un-metered journey), do agree on the price before setting out; all taxi-drivers should carry an official price list.

Coach tours are the most popular way of seeing the island, and convoys of tourist-laden coaches converge onto the roads during the summer season, much to the frustration of the local drivers (and tourists in hired cars). However, you can get to know the island comfortably in this way, before embarking on your own adventures.

The most economical way of getting about is by local transport — frequent **train** services on the Palma/Inca/Sa Pobla line, with bus connections to Lluc, Alcúdia, Pollença, etc (http://tib.caib.es); the 'wild-west' **narrow-gauge railway** between Palma and Sóller (www.trendesoller.com); the tram between Sóller and the Port, and the local **bus** network (http://tib.caib.es). All these public transport systems are economical, reliable — and fun! The Sóller train is one of the island's best-known tourist attractions. But the train between Palma and Inca is also amusing: the run is a flat one across the plain, and the train hurtles along like a bullet. Remember, too, that you'll have very good views perched up on bus seats and that, generally, the buses are new and very comfortable. (Note that outside Palma you can flag down a bus anywhere along its route, without making for the centre of a village.)

The following two pages show bus and train departure points in Palma. Bus stops and taxi ranks in Sóller are indicated on the town plan on page 95. On pages 131-133 you'll find public transport timetables current at the time of writing, but *please do not rely solely on the timetables in this book;* changes to timetables are fairly frequent. Obtain a listing from the nearest tourist office as soon as you arrive on the island. Finally, do remember that local transport will be much busier on Sundays and holidays.

KEY

1 Tourist offices (three locations)	13 Sollerich Palace
2 Town hall	14 Almundaina Palace
3 Police	15 La Lonja
4 Post office	16 Maritime museum
5 Sant Pere Bastion	17 Club Nàutic (Yacht club)
6 Flea market	18 Sta Eulalia
7 Museum (arts and crafts)	19 Sant Françesc
8 Mallorca Museum	20 Market
9 Marqués de Palmer Palace	21 Hospital
10 Arab baths	🚕 Taxi ranks
11 Episcopal Palace museum)	🚗 Petrol stations
12 Cathedral	P Parking

Transport departure points

All trains depart from the stations at the Parc de les Estacions (🚂).
All buses depart from the bus station at the Parc de les Estacions (🚌) and leav
    Palma via C/Eusebio Estada.

Useful addresses/telephone numbers

Tourist office, Palma (Sant Domingo 11): 971-724090
Tourist information office, Parc de les Estacions: 971-754329
Mallorca Tourist Board, C/Constitució No 1, 1st floor: 971-725396
Tourist information office, airport: 971-789556
Tourist office, Sóller (Plaça de Sa Constitució): 971-630200
Tourist office, Port de Sóller (Canonge Oliver, 10): 971-633042

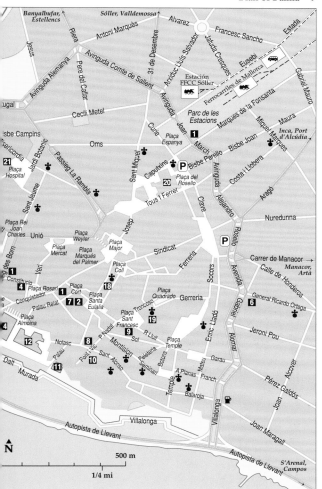

Tourist office, Pollença (Sant Domingo 2): 971-535077
Tourist office, Port de Pollença (Carretera de Formentor 31): 971-865447
Tourist office, Valldemossa (Cartuja de Valldemossa): 971-612106
Railway stations, Parc de les Estacions
   Trains to Sóller: 971-752051 or 971-752028
   Trains to Inca/Sa Pobla: 971-752245
Bus routing information (Parc de les Estacions): 971-176970
Central hotel/apartment reservations: 971-706006
Farm holidays *(agroturismo)* (Av. Gabriel Villalonga, 8A, 2nd floor):
   Tel 971-721508; Fax 971-717317
Emergency/search and rescue/forest fires, etc: 112
IBANAT (Institut Balear de la Natura), Gran Vía Asima 4: 971-177564,
   971-431782

Picnicking

Picnicking can be great fun on Mallorca, providing that you choose either an established picnic site created by IBANAT or an open area along the course of one of the walks. Much of Mallorca's land is in private hands — although it might appear to be open countryside. So never cross fences or picnic in enclosed fields, or you might find yourselves confronted by an irate landowner!

Our Forestry Commission, the Institut BAlear de la NATura (IBANAT) administers several beauty spots as areas for public enjoyment. These sites with tables (and often other facilities) are indicated both in the car touring notes and on the touring map by the symbol ⊼. However, if you prefer a 'get away from it all' picnic — or if you find that the established sites are too crowded (possible in the summer and on Sundays and holidays) — why not try a picnic spot along the route of one of the walks?

All the information you need to get to these 'private' picnics is given on the following pages, where *picnic numbers correspond to walk numbers,* so that you can quickly find the general location on the island by looking at the touring map (where the area of each walk is highlighted). Under each picnic description, you'll find walking times, a map reference, and transport details (🚌, 🚐: how to get there by bus or train; 🚗: car or taxi parking). The exact location of the picnic spot is shown on the appropriate *walking map* by the symbol *P* printed in green. To help you choose an appealing setting, photographs are included for many of the picnic suggestions.

Please remember that these picnics are 'off the beaten track': wear sensible shoes and take a **sunhat** (○ alerts you to a picnic spot in full sun). It's a good idea to take along a plastic sheet as well, in case the ground is damp or prickly. **If you're travelling to your picnic by public transport**, refer to the timetables on pages 131-133, but do remember to pick up the latest timetables once you arrive on the island. **If you are travelling by car**, watch out for animals and children on the

Torre de Cala Embasset (Picnic 1)

country roads, and always drive very carefully through villages. Without damaging plants, do park well off the road; *never* block a road or track.

All picnickers should read the country code on page 48 and go quietly in the countryside.

1 Torre de Cala Embasset (*map page 60, photograph opposite*)

🚌 to Sant Elm; 45min on foot. Or 🚗 to Sant Elm; 30min on foot. Use notes for Walk 1 (page 58) to walk or drive to Ca'n Tomeví, where there is room to park just a couple of cars alongside the fence. Go left past the fenced-off area, following the sandy track. Continue along the signposted path, coming up onto a wide track that ascends from Sant Elm. Turn right and keep up to the top of the rise. When the track ends, go right, following a narrow earthen path through the woods (waymarked with red paint daubs). Later the path descends gently towards the ancient watchtower perched on the cliff-edge above the beach of Cala Embasset. Return the same way if you parked at Ca'n Tomeví; otherwise follow the wide track (or the somewhat vertiginous cliff-hugging path) directly to Sant Elm.

2 Puig Basset (*map page 60*) ○

🚌 to S'Arracó (ask for the cemetery 1km past the village) or 🚗 (to KM5) at S'Arracó; 1h on foot. Follow Short walk 2 on page 62 to the rocky brow of the mountain. Magnificent views towards Dragonera and over the southwest coast!

3 Estellencs overlook (*map page 65*) ○

🚗 Only accessible by car; 30min on foot. See Walk 3, page 64: drive to the Font d'es Pí and then follow Walk 3 for 30min. Wonderful views down over

Estellencs on the coast, from the flanks of Galatzó — mostly in full sun, but with a little shade on the rocky outcrop.

6 Son Fortuny (*map page 64*) 🗔

🚗 Only accessible by car; 25min on foot. Drive to KM97 on the Ma-10 and park well off the road. Follow Walk 6 (page 71) for 25min. Son Fortuny is a beautiful, peaceful picnic area in the quiet woodlands of the northern foothills below Galatzó. Tables, benches; plenty of shade.

7 Puig de Santa Eugènia (*map page 76, photographs pages 13 and 76*) ○

🚌 or 🚗 to Santa Eugènia; 25min on foot. Walk up to the main square with the fountain, the Plaça de Bernardo de Santa Eugènia, and continue up the steep hill by the side of the 'Correos' (post office). Once up onto the level tarmac lane at the top, turn right and walk to the end, then go left up the stony, walled-in track. Where this ends, go through the gap in the wall, to follow a narrow earthen path up to the top of the hill. Go over the low wall by the side of an old pine, and on up to the cross monument. An excellent viewpoint — almost the entire island is visible! No shade. Can be very windy in winter.

8 So Na Rossa (*map page 77*) 🗔

🚌 or 🚗 to Santa Eugènia (drive to the end of the village, towards Algaida, and park in the lane on the right, by the orchard wall — as described in Walk 8 on page 77); 55min on foot. Follow Walk 8 on

Orient Valley (Picnic 14)

page 77 for 50min, then turn down left. Walk down the narrow lane for about five minutes and, just after a sharp bend to the left, you will come to a well-landscaped picnic spot with tables, benches and barbecues. (You can also park in Biniali or take a bus to Biniali and walk over the bridge and down the lane to this picnic spot in 5-7 minutes.)

9 Font d'es Polls (*map page 82*) ⊞

🚌 or 🚶 to Valldemossa; 50min on foot. Follow Short walk 2 (page 79) as far as the picnic site, by an old well. Wooden tables and benches. Plenty of shade from the poplars (*polls*), but no views.

10 Valldemossa overlook
(*map page 82, photograph of Valldemossa page 22*)

🚌 or 🚶 to Valldemossa; 1h20min on foot. This is a very long walk for a picnic, but I wanted to include this in the picnic section because of its spectacular position! Follow Walk 10b on page 83 as far as the viewpoint — *not* the first rocky outcrop after the bend, but the *second* one, a little further along, where a narrow stone-edged path (marked by a small red arrow at ground level) leads off right to a natural 'platform'. Stunning panoramic views over Valldemossa

and the surrounding mountains, down as far as the coast and Palma city. Sun or shade.

13 Font de Ses Mentides
(*map page 88*) ○

🚌 or 🚶 to Deià; 40min on foot. Follow the Shorter walk on page 88 to the stone steps just beyond the hamlet of Son Coll, and turn left down to the mountain spring (signposted), where you can picnic on a stone seat by the small pool. (If there are several walkers about, space here may be limited, so after visiting the spring, picnic on the wide steps.) Little shade; no far-reaching views.

14 Orient Valley (*map page 91, photograph above*) ○

🚶 Only accessible by car; 30min on foot. Park at KM11.9 on the Alaró/Orient road, or nearby, well off the road. Follow Walk 14 (page 90) for 30min, to picnic on the small grassy outcrop. Panoramic views down over the peaceful Orient Valley. Mostly in sun, but there is a shady clearing a little further up.

16 Es Barranc (*map on reverse of touring map, photograph page 98*)

🚶 to Biniaraix; 10-15min on foot. Or 🚌 or 🚃 to Sóller; 45min on foot (but consider taking a taxi to from Sóller to Biniaraix, then you will only have to walk for 15min). Follow Walk 16 on page 95 as far as the 45min-point — or further; choose a picnic spot anywhere along Es Barranc, in sun or shade.

18 Sa Font de Bálitx *(map on reverse of touring map, nearby photograph page 100)*

🚌 *(restricted timetable)* or 🚗 to the Mirador de Ses Barques; 35min on foot. Follow Walk 18 (page 99) for 35min, to picnic by the mountain spring or on the grassy terrace nearby. Sun or shade. Lovely valley views on the way.

19 Sa Calobra *(map on reverse of touring map, photograph page 102)* ○

🚗, 🚌 or ⛴ to Sa Calobra; 15-20min on foot. Walk through the tunnels (take care; the surface underfoot is uneven) to the shingle beach, and explore as far as you like up the Pareis Gorge; there are many good picnic spots, but little shade. Do not attempt to venture beyond the first large boulders without adequate climbing equipment.

20 Cúber Lake *(map on reverse of touring map, overview photograph page 107, top)* ○

🚌 *(restricted timetable)* or 🚗 to the Cúber Lake; 10-30min on foot. Leave your transport at the small parking area at KM34 on the Ma-10, by the Cúber Lake. Go through the access gate; there are plenty of grassy picnic spots off the track only a few minutes downhill, with expansive views across the lake to the surrounding

mountain peaks. There is also an IBANAT stone refuge with a picnic table and bench at the far end of the lake (30min on foot), which may be used if no one is staying at the refuge. This is a spectacular spot, with impressive views of the lake and the Puig Major. The area is also a bird-watchers' paradise. No shade, except at the refuge.

21 Gorg Blau overlook *(map on reverse of touring map, nearby photograph page 105)* ○

🚌 *(restricted timetable)* or 🚗 to the Cúber Lake (park as for Picnic 20); 15-30min on foot. Follow Walk 21 (page 105), taking the maintenance path alongside the watercourse as far as you like. There are several good picnic spots along the way, on rocky outcrops, with superb views down over the Gorg Blau lake hidden between the island's two highest mountains — Massanella and the Puig Major. Little shade.

22 Font d'es Prat de Massanella *(map on reverse of touring map, photographs pages 54, 105, 107, bottom)*

🚌 *(restricted timetable)* or 🚗 to the Cúber Lake; 1h15min on foot. Follow *Walk 21* (page 105), taking the maintenance path alongside the watercourse, but continue over the bridge, following the text as far as the 1h05min-point. Then pick up notes for Walk 22, page 108, to go to the Font d'es Prat. Picnic in the shady clearing by the spring. No far-reaching views at the picnic spot, but plenty along the way!

The plain from the Puig de Santa Eugènia (Picnic 7)

24a Lluc Valley overlook (map on reverse of touring map, nearby photographs page 110)

🚌 or 🚗 to Lluc monastery; 15-20min on foot. Go to the left of the monastery building, and walk up the wide steps; a shady trail leads up to the top of the hill by the cross monument. Plenty of sunny or shady spots for picnicking, with excellent views over the valley and the monastery.

24b Lluc (map on reverse of touring map, nearby photographs page 110) 🏕

🚌 or 🚗 to Lluc monastery; 5-20min on foot. There are many lovely picnic areas in and around Lluc, with sun, shade, and drinking fountains; there's a good picnic spot directly in front of the car park at Lluc itself. But why not follow Walk 24 (page 114) and picnic somewhere along the picturesque old track, or by the camping site where you can use the barbecues? It's only about 20min along.

24c Binibona (map page 113)

🚌 to Caimari; 40min on foot, or 🚗 to Binibona; 15-20min on foot. Walk or drive along the quiet country lane from Caimari to the wide square in Binibona (park well tucked in). Then follow the track off left at the far end of the square into the woods for as long as you like. About fifteen minutes along here, you can cross the stream bed down to the right, to find a good picnic spot.

24d Binifaldó (map on reverse of touring map)

🚌 or 🚗 to Lluc monastery; 30-50min on foot. Follow Walk 24 (page 114), and turn into the old route towards Binifaldó. Follow it as far as you like; there are many good picnic spots along the way, where weathered limestone rocks form natural 'tables', in sun or in shade. (Note: If you are travelling by car, the gates to the Binifaldó water-bottling plant are open Mondays to Fridays, saving you 20-25min walking. Turn in at the KM17.4 marker on the Ma-10 and park by the gates at Menut, well off the side of the lane, or go through the gates and park less than 2km along, below the big house of Binifaldó at the foot of Tomir.)

IBANAT picnic sites (map on reverse of touring map, nearby photograph page 119) 🏕

🚌 (restricted timetable) or 🚗 to KM16.5 on the Ma-10; up to 15min on foot. There are two options: either park inside the picnic grounds (with barbecues, running water, WCs, swing park, etc), or continue down the road for 100m/yds to KM16.4. Here you can walk through the wooden gate and follow a wide track through the woods for about 15min. You will come to a small spring (on a bend to the left), and a more secluded stone refuge higher up. There are also a couple of picnic sites on the opposite side of the road, one at KM16.4 and another further along at KM17.4. Note: IBANAT picnic sites are only crowded on local fiesta days or at weekends. All sites offer sun and shade.

28 Bóquer Valley (map page 123, photograph opposite)

🚌 to Port de Pollença; 35-45min on foot, or 🚗 to the Oro Playa apartments at Port de Pollença on the Ma-2210 to Formentor (park opposite the tree-lined avenue up to the Bóquer farm); 20-30min on foot. Follow Walk 28 on page 123, to head up into the Bóquer

Valley, and either picnic at the 'wild west ambush scene' amongst the fallen rocks and boulders for shade, or further along the route in the open valley, in full sun. Beautiful views on all sides.

29a La Victoria viewpoint *(map page 126, nearby photograph page 125, bottom)* ○

🚗 to the Ermita de la Victoria; 3min on foot. (You can also take a 🚌 to Alcúdia and then a taxi to the Ermita de la Victoria; remember to arrange a return pick-up time with the taxi driver.) From the car park by the old church at the *ermita,* go left down a few steps and then straight ahead, following a narrow path through the trees. It leads in a couple of minutes to a magnificent viewpoint protected by a wooden fence and complete with some seating, overlooking the Bay of Pollença and the distant mountains of the Formentor Peninsula. Full sun.

29b Alcúdia overlook *(map page 126, nearby photographs page 125, middle and bottom)* ○

🚗 or 🚌 as 29a above; 30min on foot. Follow Walk 29 on page 124, but ignore the path to Penya Rotja. Continue up the main track to just past the wide barred gate, and picnic on a platform on the right (just where the track levels out). Magnificent views down over the Bay of Pollença. There is no shade here, but there are some trees a little further along the track.

29c Coll Baix *(map page 126, photograph page 125, top)* 🏕

🚗 Only accessible by car; 5min on foot. Drive from Alcúdia towards Mal Pas, and turn right by the Bodega del Sol bar, to follow the tarmac lane into the Victoria Park. Keep along for some time, and

Bóquer Valley (Picnic 28)

park at the wide parking area just after some steep bends. A five minute walk will bring you to the picnic site at a pass at the end of the road, the Coll Baix. There is plenty of shade, a stone refuge, tables and benches, and a drinking fountain. Or picnic down at Coll Baix Beach (35min on foot): descend the wide path from the picnic site — you will have to scramble over large boulders at the end (not ideal if you are carrying a heavy picnic bag).

31 Cala Malsoc *(map page 127, photograph page 128)*

🚗 Only accessible by car; 30min on foot. See page 127: 'How to get there' and drive to Cala Estreta to park. Then follow Walk 31 as far as Cala Malsoc, to picnic in sun or shade, in this lovely sandy cove bordered by pine woods. Beautiful sea views.

32 Cala Beltrán *(map page 129)*

🚌 or 🚗 to Cala Pí; 25min on foot. Follow Walk 32 (page 129) to Cala Beltrán. There's ample sun on the cliff-tops or shade and privacy in this sheltered little cove.

❊ Touring

The ideal way to tour Mallorca is by car, of course. Most of
the island's roads are in very good condition, although there
are a lot of roadworks in progress as this Sixth edition goes
to press. The mountainous northwest coast is the most
popular side of the island, with spectacular scenery that you
must not miss. The east coast has its own distinct flavour, and
touring here is especially enjoyable in spring or summer,
months when you can take advantage of the idyllic beaches.

Car hire

Remember that it's wise to shop around, because car
hire prices vary quite a bit. As a generalisation, prices at the
local firms are lower than those of international chains. Be
sure that you understand the terms of the hire agreement that
you have signed and what the insurance covers. You will need
a current driving licence, and *only* those people whose licence
numbers and names have been written on the agreement will
be covered by insurance to drive the car. *Do* check the car
carefully for damage before you take it on the road. You will
also be expected to pay a (cash) deposit against insurance and
may be asked to pay for petrol when you sign the agreement
(which will be refunded if you return the car with a full tank).
Most of the 24-hour service stations are located in Palma;
outside the capital, many petrol stations close at 2pm on
Sundays and holidays.

Motoring laws

All road signs on Mallorca are international, except
for the 'give way' sign, which reads *ceda el paso*. The motoring
laws below are strictly enforced:

- **Right of way** must be given to any vehicle coming from your right,
  except at roundabouts and where otherwise indicated;
- All passengers must wear **seat belts**, and children are not permitted
  in the front seats until they are old enough to wear seat belts;
- **Unbroken lines** in the centre of the road must not be crossed;
- **Three-point turns** and **reversing** into side streets are forbidden in
  built-up areas;
- **Parking** facing oncoming traffic is prohibited, as is parking on any
  very narrow or one-way roads;
- You must display a **parking permit** in all 'blue' zones — fines for
  failure to do so are high (purchase tickets from the machines; be sure
  to carry enough change);

- **Speed limits** vary, at the time of writing: 120km/h on motorways, 100km/h on main and secondary roads, 90km/h on other roads, and 40km/h (unless otherwise indicated) in towns and villages.

When planning your tour, remember that you won't cover more than about 35km per hour on the winding mountain roads. Always **allow for delays** along some of the main and mountain roads during the summer season, and especially on Sundays, when all the 'weekenders' are returning to Palma. And **allow plenty of time for stops**; the driving times given only include short breaks at the viewpoints labelled (🕭) in the text. Most of the larger villages have **repair garages**; these are often next to the petrol station. There are **telephones** in nearly all villages, usually in the main square. **Toilet facilities** are found at bar-cafés and restaurants, most petrol stations, and at major tourist attractions. Apart from the emergency medical centres shown in the notes and on the touring map (⊕), many beaches have **first-aid kiosks** *in summer*.

The touring notes

The six excursions described all fan out from the capital, covering the island in clockwise fashion. The outer ring road circling Palma provides easy access from the city to the mountains, as does the motorway to Inca (and eventually Alcúdia).

The notes themselves are very brief: they include little material that you can obtain free in leaflets available from tourist information kiosks. Instead, I've concentrated on the 'logistics' of touring: times and distances, road conditions, facilities en route, etc. Most of all, these notes emphasise possibilities for **walking** and **picnicking**.

Important: At time of writing, bypass roads are being built around several towns and *all roads are being renumbered*. If you come to a roundabout not mentioned in the notes, follow the signposts to your next destination. *We use the new road numbers in our text and on our maps,* although some roads may not yet be renumbered 'on the ground'.

The fold-out touring map is designed to be held out opposite the touring notes and contains all the information you should need outside Palma; the city exits are shown on the Palma town plan on pages 8-9.

Various **symbols** have been used in the notes and on the touring map, to alert you to attractions and facilities en route at a glance; refer to the map key.

For a two-day tour, consider staying overnight at one of the island's **monasteries**: see pages 47-48; they are inexpensive and beautifully-sited.

1 SPECTACULAR SOUTHWEST SETTINGS

Palma • Peguera (Cala Fornells) • Camp de Mar • Port d'Andratx •
Sant Elm • Andratx • Estellencs • Banyalbufar • La Granja (Esporles)
• Puigpunyent • La Reserva de Galatzó • Palma

120km/74mi; 4h driving
On route: ⊼ at Galatzó Nature
Reserve; Picnics (see pages 10-
15): 1, 2, (3), 6; also Caló d'en
Monjo, a short walk from Cala
Fornells; Walks: 1, 2, (3), 4, 5, 6
Opening hours/market days
La Granja (tel: 971-610032) is
open daily from 10.00-19.00;
exhibition of Mallorcan folk

dancing in typical costume Wednesdays and Fridays at 16:00 and
17:00. **La Reserva de Galatzó**
(tel: 971-616622) is open daily
from 09.30-18.00 in winter and
from 09.30-19.00 in summer
(tickets can be purchased up to
two hours before closing time).
Market in Andratx: Wednesday
mornings

A leisurely, all-day tour with plenty of interesting places to
see. Remember to allow a couple of hours' daylight at
the end to enjoy the Galatzó Nature Reserve. The roads are
good, but narrow and winding (even tortuous) between
Andratx and Puigpunyent. At time of writing the Ma-1
motorway is being extended to Port d'Andratx.

Leave Palma by driving west along
the beautiful, palm-shaded Passeig
Marítim, passing the Club Nàutic,
where many expensive yachts
moor, and the commercial port
and naval zone of Porto Pí. The
motorway continues ahead
(signposted to Andratx) and
climbs gradually above the resort
of Cala Major, hidden by high-rise
apartment blocks. Soon, the
Castell de Bendinat★ (8km ■)
appears on the left — a beautiful
neo-Gothic palace surrounded by
parklands, now privately owned

and closed to the public; below it
is the Bendinat Golf Club. Further
along you pass by the resorts of
Illetes, Portals Nous with its
Marineland aquarium, and Palma
Nova. Continue along the Ma-1
motorway, passing turn-offs to
Mallorc's casino, Magaluf and
Santa Ponça (keep straight ahead
at the flyover and roundabout).
Soon you come to Peguera
(20km), but continue along the
main road through two tunnels
(Peguera's promenade has now
been pedestrianised, and it is

Fishing nets drying near the cathedral in Palma make a colourful display

better to enter at the far end to avoid a confusing drive through the back streets). Leave at Exit 3, signposted to Cala Fornells, to go left above the main road. Go right at the roundabout and continue straight down, passing two traffic lights, coming into **Peguera** (📷✕🏨⊕) at a roundabout on the old main through road, where you can park and explore on foot.

To continue, go right (west) along the road and, at the next roundabout, go left and up over a steep hill. At the bottom turn right to **Cala Fornells★** (24.5km 📷✕), one of the island's prettiest coves, with small white beaches and rocky inlets. You can park at the end of the road, up a wide sandy track. (For a more secluded cove, walk up the track for about ten minutes, veering left and wind down to Caló d'en Monjo, absolutely idyllic and perfect for a picnic.)

Return to the roundabout (25.5km) and go left out of Peguera along the main road. Shortly, turn left on the Ma-1010 leading down to **Camp de Mar** (28km 📷✕⊕). At the first roundabout head west on the Ma-1020, to wind up over pine-covered hills and down into scenic **Port d'Andratx** (33km 📷✕🏨). There are two municipal car parks which make for easy parking, so you can wander through the narrow streets at leisure, or take some refreshment at one of the port-side cafés. Or you can drive up onto Sa Mola (signposted) to admire the views across to the Isle of Dragonera which you'll see later today.

Leaving this picturesque harbour scene behind you, take the wide road out of the port for just under 3km. Go left on the Ma-1022, then right at the roundabout on the Ma-1050, following signs to Sant Elm. You come into **S'Arracò** (38km ✕P2), where

Walk 2 and Short walk 2 begin and end. Go left at the round-about, out of the village, to wind up over more thickly wooded hills. The Ma-1030 takes you down into **Sant Elm** (42km 📷✕P1) — a quiet fishing village in winter, a peaceful resort in summer. The streets are pedestrianised, but there is ample parking at the entrance on the right.

For a good view to the Isle of Dragonera across the blue straits, or to reach the port, Walk 1 and the watchtower, continue driving past the car park: wind up the hill to the right and curve round behind the resort, passing signposts to 'Torre de Cala Embasset, Sa Trapa, Parc Natural de Sa Dragonera'. The second turning left will bring you to the far end of the port, for good fish restaurants overlooking the islet and easy parking. There are also boat trips across to Sa Dragonera most of the year.

Return to S'Arracò and keep ahead at the roundabout, to drive over the hill into **Andratx** (49km ✝📷✕🏨⊕), where there is a colourful market on Wednesday mornings. Follow the narrow street, going right along the one-way system, and take the second right, signposted to Estellencs, Palma and Sóller. After several 'no-entry's, take the next viable left turn, past a small square, and turn right on the main road. Then take the next left, the Ma-10, sign-posted to Estellencs.

Now wind up through a green landscape of pine-clad hills and mountains, towards the rugged western coastline of steep cliffs and rocky inlets. The road continues through two tunnels, and soon you come to the cliff-top restaurant of Es Grau (63km ✕) and the adjoining **Mirador de Ricardo Roca★** (📷). The stone steps lead up to a precarious viewpoint and stone shelter (a good place to

picnic), with splendid panoramic views along this wild stretch of coastline.

The Ma-10 now dives down through the small tunnel of Es Grau and hugs the coast. At the KM97 marker you pass a stony track on the right: it leads to a magnificent picnic area with barbecues up in the woods (**P6**) and is also the starting point for Walks 5 and 6. At the **Coll d'es Pí** (65km ✕🍴🔭) the road turns inland and down into **Estellencs** (67km ✝🏔✕⊕). This delightful mountain village sits at the foot of Mount Galatzó, setting for Walks 3-5. The fertile, terraced slopes, irrigated by channelled mountain springs, are studded with orange groves and olive trees. The road narrows somewhat as it leaves the village and snakes its way to the **Talaia de Ses Animes**★ (72km 🔭; photograph page 70), a renovated watchtower where you can park and cross the bridge for more magnificent coastal views, especially of the sloping cultivated terraces shown above. Next you come to **Banyalbufar** (74km 🏔✕⊕), set on slopes above the sea. It's worth turning down sharp left in front of the Hotel Mar i Vent and following the narrow streets downhill; there's a parking

20

area further down, and one can visit a quaint little cemetery overlooking the sea.

From here the road swings inland once more, passing the turn-off to Port d'Es Canonge (81km), a picturesque little fishing port way down on the rocks, and continues over the hills through thick pine forests. At the next junction, keep straight on for Esporles along the Ma-1100, and then turn right on the Ma-1101 (83km; signposted to Puigpunyent). On the left is the entrance to **La Granja**★. This large, splendid mansion once belonged to the Cistercian monks and later to an aristocratic Mallorcan family, but the archways and ornamental fountains evoke its Moorish past. It is certainly worth a visit.

From La Granja continue along the narrow and twisting road over the hill and come down in sharp S-bends to the pretty mountain village of **Puigpunyent** (93km 🏔✕; Walk 4). Follow the one-way system down to the bottom and turn right towards 'Galilea', keeping straight ahead at the junction. Coming up the rise out of the village, turn right and follow the 'La Reserva' signs (see detailed map on page 65). Soon the road begins to climb in endless bends, passing the turn-off right to the Font d'es Pí (**P3** and Walk 3.) Eventually you arrive at the Galatzó Nature Reserve, **La Reserva**★ (101km 🍴). With its 30 waterfalls, bridges, bears and other animals, luxuriant vegetation and mountain scenery, it's a nature-lovers' paradise.

Back in Puigpunyent, turn right at the junction for Palma. Enter the city (120km) by keeping ahead at both roundabouts, or go left or right at second roundabout onto the ring road, to find your exit.

2 PRETTY MOUNTAIN VILLAGES

Palma • Valldemossa • Costa Nord • Port de Valldemossa • Ermita de Sa Trinitat • Son Marroig • Deià • Port de Sóller • Balearic Museum of Natural Science (Sóller) • Gardens of Alfabia • Palma

90km/56mi; 4h driving

On route: ♨ at the Ermita de Sa Trinitat and Son Marroig; Picnics (see pages 10-15): 9, 10, 12, 13; Walks: 9, 10, 11, 12, 13

Opening hours/market days
The **Carthusian Monastery** (Valldemossa; tel: 971-612106) is open daily March-October from 09.30-18.00 (Sundays 13.00), November-February from 09.30-16.30 (Sundays 13.00). Closed Christmas Day. Live piano recitals (Chopin, of course!) hourly until 16.30 from Monday to Saturday and on Sunday mornings.
Costa Nord (Valldemossa; tel: 971-612425) is open daily from 09:00-15:00 (Monday); 09.00-17:00 (Tuesday-Sunday). Traditional Mallorcan folk dancing on Tuesdays, Wednesdays and Fridays at 10.00 and 12.30.
Miramar (tel: 971 616073) is open all year round from 10.00-18.00; closed Mondays.
Son Marroig (Deià; tel: 971-639158) is open from 09:30-20.00 in summer; 09.30-18:00 in winter; closed Sundays. Summer concerts are held during August and September.
Archaeological Museum of Deià (tel: 971-639001) is open daily.
The **Balearic Museum of Natural Science and Botanical Gardens** (Sóller; tel: 971-634064) are open Tuesday-Saturday from 10.00-18.00; Sundays and public holidays 10.00-14.00; closed Mondays.
The **Gardens of Alfabia** (tel: 971-613123) are open from 09:30-18:30 Monday-Friday; 09.30-13.00 Saturdays; closed Sundays.
Market in Sóller: Saturday mornings

I suggest you make a full day of this short tour, as there are so many interesting places to visit along the way. The roads are mostly good, although mountainous. The road down to Port de Valldemossa is especially narrow and tortuous.

From Palma's ring road (Vía Cintura; Ma-20,) take the exit to Valldemossa, and at the round-about keep ahead on the Ma-1110 (🚌), heading north towards the mountain range through almond orchards and farmlands. The glass-blowing factory just past **S'Esgleieta** (8km) makes an interesting stop-off if you set out early enough. Soon the road starts to climb gradually between slopes clad with olive trees towards the picturesque mountain village where Chopin and George Sand spent the winter of 1838-9; the blue-tiled bell tower of the monastery where they rented cells is clearly visible from the road as you wind up towards the mountains.

Come into **Valldemossa★** (16km ♘♠✕⊕M*P*9, 10), where you can park at any of the paying car parks on the main road. Or, to park free, turn right just after the pedestrian crossing and park on any of the side streets near Son Gual, the big house with a square tower just behind the main road. Visit Valldemossa on foot: cross the main road and follow the narrow cobbled streets to the square and the monastery. A ticket to the monastery includes a visit to Chopin's quarters (containing one of his pianos, his death mask, and some original manuscripts, letters and documents), a very interesting 17th-century pharmacy, various exhibits (including one of

The bell tower of the monastery rises above Valldemossa. Originally the site of a Moorish palace, the buildings were later the retreat of King Sancho. After his death, the palace was given to the Carthusian monks who, little by little, constructed the monastery. When this religious order was expelled from Spain in 1835, private owners took over and rented the cells to travellers — including the poet Ruben Darío and the writers Unamuno and Azorín.

Europe's oldest printing presses), art collections, and the palace of King Sancho (where the live piano recitals are held). Nearby tourist shops sell carved olive-wood objects and hand-embroidered shawls. A visit to **Costa Nord**, located on the main road opposite the car park, is a must. Michael Douglas takes you on an historical tour of the island, and you later visit the interior of the Archduke Luis Salvador's yacht, the 'Nixe', for a fascinating *son et lumière*. The visit ends at a thematic exhibition full of books, drawings, photographs, maps, and other memorabilia. There are also folk dancing performances; see page 21. Walks 9 and 10 are based on Valldemossa.

Leave the village in direction of Andratx/Sóller (signposted). You will see the large old house of Son Moragues with its stone arches up to the right just outside Vallde-mossa; this was one of the Archduke Luis Salvador of Austria's many mansions. Pass the turn-off right to Deià (19km; Ma-10, and some 400m further along turn right on the Ma-1131

leading down to Valldemossa's port. *Please drive carefully* down this narrow, tortuous road cut into the cliff. **Port de Valldemossa** (24km ✕), surrounded by high red cliffs, is a quaint little fishing hamlet sitting on the rocks, where several more modern dwellings have sprung up over the last few years.

Return to the Ma-10 and keep left towards Deià (✉ at 30km). It is not long before you pass a right turn signposted 'Ermita'; the sign is hidden from view on the approach, and the track is best accessed by turning left into the C'an Costa restaurant a few metres further on and then doubling back. The 1km-long track, *very narrow in places*, rises to the **Ermita de Sa Trinitat** (32.5km ✚⋒☕). There is plenty of room to park and turn around at the top. Visit the tiny chapel and the small interior patio — from where you can enjoy a superb coastal view. There is also a delightful picnic area under the trees. (If you don't fancy driving up, park at C'an Costa and walk up.)

Again rejoining the Ma-10, after passing an isolated holiday apartment block, come to the entrance down to **Miramar★** (36km), founded by Ramon Llull in 1276 and an early acquisition of the Archduke Luis Salvador. One can see a very old olive press and explore the house — full of interesting objects and art, some of the navigation equipment used on his yacht, the 'Nixe', and the garden with its original archways dating from the days of Ramon Llull. Continuing along the Ma-10 you will soon come to **Son Marroig Son Marroig**★ (38km ✻☞M), the archduke's principal residence. There's good parking and *miradors* from which to view the famous rock, Sa Foradada, pierced with a hole. After looking at the marble *mirador* in the gardens, go into the house; a tour of the rooms containing the original furniture, several of his excellent sketches and paintings, writings, portraits and photographs of his family, amply repays the small entrance fee. Luis Salvador's exceptional love for Mallorcan natural history is very much in evidence. You could also walk down to Sa Foradada.

Continue along the coast to the incredibly picturesque mountain village of **Deià**★ (40.5km ✝☎ ✻M; photograph page 85), home of many well-known artists and poets — Robert Graves being one of the earliest to settle here. Visit, perhaps, the small but interesting archeological museum and the little church on the hilltop with a charming cemetery, where you can find Robert Graves' tombstone. Walks 11 and 13 are based on Deià.

At the village exit you pass La Residencia, a luxury hotel, and about 1km out of Deià a little road leads off left down to the shingle beach at Cala de Deià (Walk 11). At KM60.2 you pass the starting point for Walk 13 and its shorter version (*P*13), then the road contours above Lluc-Alcari (44km ☎✻), another artists' colony you might like to visit (✻ at 46km) — perhaps on foot (Alternative walk 11). Soon (47km) a road off left on a sharp bend signposted 'Bens D'Avall' leads down in interminable bends to one of the most

splendidly situated restaurants on the island.

Continuing along the Ma-10, more splendid views unfold: the distant high peaks of the Puig Major and lower mountains surrounding the Sóller basin, where a myriad of citrus and olive groves populate the pine-clad slopes. On coming to the main road (Ma-11) in the valley, turn left and head for **Port de Sóller** (54km ☎✻). Here amidst sun-seekers, seaside restaurants and crowded beaches, the summer comes into its own. On the other hand, it's rather desolate in winter. Returning along the Ma-11 (⛽ at 59km), just past the petrol station you'll find the **Balearic Museum of Natural Science** (M with **Botanical Gardens**) on the left, with plenty of parking space. From the outskirts of Sóller your homeward route now snakes uphill in interminable bends towards the mountain pass.* A superb view down over the Sóller valley can be seen at the *mirador*★ (☎) almost at the top, and on the south side of the **Coll de Sóller** (66km) you soon come to another viewpoint by a mountain-top café (67km ✻☎), this time over-looking Palma's bay.

Winding down the mountainside through endless olive terracing, you reach a roundabout at the exit from the Sóller tunnel. Circle round and back north, *past* the Palma road. Now you can stretch your legs again at the **Gardens of Alfabia**★ (73km ✿✻), while you explore the exotic pavilions, romantic arbours and bamboo-shaded lily ponds. The final stretch (⛽ 88km) returns you to Palma (90km).

---

*If it is late in the day, you can avoid this tortuous mountain route by going straight through the Sóller tunnel (a toll is payable).

3 THE MAGNIFICENT MOUNTAIN ROUTE AND THE CAPES

Palma • Sóller • Biniaraix • Mirador de Ses Barques • Cúber and Gorg Blau lakes • Sa Calobra • Lluc • Pollença • Port de Pollença • Cap de Formentor • Alcúdia • Cap d'es Pinar • Port d'Alcúdia • Coves de Campanet • Palma

235km/146mi; 8h driving (a two-day tour)

On route: Ħ at the Mirador de Ses Barques, Sa Bassa, Cúber Lake, Lluc, Ma-10 at KM16.4, Ermita de la Victoria; Picnics (see pages 10-15): (14), 16, 18-22, 24a, 24b, (24c), 24d, 26-29; Walks: (13-16), 12, 17-29

Opening hours/market days

Lluc Monastery (tel: 971-517025) is best booked in advance in summer; otherwise book at the information office on arrival; the monastery is open daily, but doors close at 23.00. The monastery's museum is open from 10.00-18.30 (April to September) and 10.00-17.30 (Oct to March).

Ca S'Amitger (Lluc, for information about the Serra de Tramuntana; tel: 971-517070) is open daily from 09.00-16.00; entrance is free.

The **Coves de Campanet** (caves; tel: 971-516130) are open daily from 10.00-19.00.

Markets — Sóller: Saturday mornings; **Pollença:** Sunday mornings; **Port de Pollença:** Wednesday mornings; **Alcúdia:** Tuesday and Sunday mornings

This beautiful two-day tour (with a night spent at Lluc monastery set in the heart of the sierra) will take you through some of the most spectacular mountain scenery on the island and is the most popular touristic route. Therefore the roads are in good condition, although you may be slowed down by traffic in summer, and you can expect to meet tourist coaches. The Ma-13A was being widened at time of writing. There are many hairpin bends on the road to Sa Calobra, although it is well surfaced.

Leave Palma's ring road (Vía Cintura) at the 'Sóller' exit, to join the Ma-11. Beyond a roundabout, the road heads straight as an arrow across the plain through dazzling pink and white almond orchards (in February) towards the sierra (✕ at 14km). Pass the entrance to the **Gardens of Alfabia★** (16km; Car tour 2), and then go straight through the (toll-paying) tunnel and down towards Sóller. At the first roundabout, keep right into the centre of **Sóller** (22km ✝▲✕⛽⊕M; Walks 13 and 16; plan page 95). This enchanting village is a popular tourist destination, not only because of its setting, but also because it's such fun to travel here on the narrow-gauge railway from Palma through the mountain and down from amazing heights. Keep straight down this narrow road and into the centre. Biniaraix and Fornalutx are signposted here, but you might first like to go left just at the tram-lines, to visit the Plaça de Sa Constitució (car park just beyond it, past the market), where you can enjoy refreshments beneath the colourful awnings of one of the cafés, or simply admire the beautiful façade of the 16th-century church shown on page 97.

Then follow signposting to Biniaraix, and cross the bridge over the stream. The narrow lane leads up past the charming little square in **Biniaraix** (24km ✝) and round to the right (photograph page 98). If you can squeeze into a parking space, you might like to explore the route of Walks 16 and 17 — a beautiful, stone-laid pilgrims' trail; it starts just opposite the road to Fornalutx, and you could follow it for five minutes (to the first little bridge; *P*16), for a lovely view of Sóller.

Continuing, follow the very narrow road towards Fornalutx, through abundant orange groves. On joining the wider Ma-2121, turn up right to **Fornalutx** (25km ♣✗⊕), one of the most picturesque villages on Mallorca. Just after passing the square (now pedestrianised) keep right to find the car park, then explore the lovely old stone-stepped streets, where open doorways show beautiful Mallorcan interiors.

Back in the car and continuing uphill, the last bar-café (opposite a car park) boasts a magnificent view down over the village and the impressive mountains that surround it. On the elevated terrace here, you can also sample one of the best *pa'amb oli*s on the island, a typical Mallorcan breakfast of local bread with olive oil, tomatoes, peppers, cured ham and green olives — very nutritious!

Leave Fornalutx now along the Ma-2120, climbing up above the village through more orange groves and olive orchards. When you meet the Ma-10, turn up right. Not long after, you come to the fabulous **Mirador de Ses Barques**★ (30km ✗🛏🖼*P*18), with astounding views down over the bay and Port of Sóller. Walk 18 starts here.

Leaving this viewpoint, continue climbing towards the peaks, with the enormous red rock mountain, the Penya d'es Migdía, looming up ahead (🛏 at Sa Bassa; 32.5km). Pass another *mirador* at the entrance to the first tunnel under the mountain, at the **Coll d'es Puig Major** (37.5km 🖼). Say goodbye to this landscape now, and take a last photograph, as you'll find the scenery completely different on the other side.

Passing a small reservoir, you wind down through the military zone of Son Torrella, and then descend a tranquil, uninhabited landscape of green valleys surrounded by rocky mountains towards a first reservoir, the **Cúber Lake** (41km 🖼*P*20-22). Many wonderful mountain hikes start here — including Alternative walk 16 and Walks 20-22. There is also a good view from here of the military base atop the magnificent rocky peak of

Landscape on the Ma-11 south of the Alfàbia Gardens, with the summits (from left to right) of Alquería, Son Nasi and Son Poc in the foreground.

the Puig Major (1445m/4740ft), the island's highest mountain. Some 2km further along, rounding the south side of Puig Major, come to the **Gorg Blau** lake (Blue Gorge; 43.5km 🍴), a second, deeper reservoir, peaceful and still, where trout fishing is allowed (with permission from IBANAT). Then you leave this enchanting valley through another tunnel. Shortly you reach the turn-off to Sa Calobra (Ma-2141; 46km; ✕), by the huge archways of a Romanesque aqueduct. The road winds up over the bare lower slopes of the Puig Major, and then loops under itself to descend a wild and rocky wilderness in a 'thousand' bends, coming to **Sa Calobra★** (58km ▲▲✕), where Walks 18 and 19 end. Leave your car at the car park some 100m up from the cove (only residents can drive through) and walk down, to see the stunning and grandiose **Torrent de Pareis★** ('Twin Torrents') — where, after heavy rains, the double torrent cascading down from the mountains between vertical cliffs almost 200m/650ft high reaches the sea at a small shingle beach. To visit this setting, shown on page 102, walk through the two tunnels cut in the rock (take care on the uneven surface underfoot). Boat trips run daily in summer (and on calm winter days), and this is decidedly the best way to see Mallorca's abrupt northern coastline.

Return to the Ma-10 and turn left towards Lluc. Soon you can stop at a viewpoint★ (73km 🍴 for the stunning 'aerial' view of the Pareis Gorge shown opposite. Further along, by the 13th-century chapel of Sant Pere (74km ✝✕) at **Escorca**, the long and tortuous footpath down into the gorge (Walk 19) begins. Keeping ahead, you eventually come to the turn-

off left to Lluc at the **Coll de Sa Bataia** (79km ✕🚌; Walks 22 and 23). Should you wish to shorten the tour to just one day, keep straight on down the Ma-2130 (**P**24c) to Inca, and return from there to Palma. But if you are game for a night at the mountain monastery and another exciting tour tomorrow, turn down left and, at the next junction, turn left to the **Santuari de Lluc★** (81km ✝▲ ✕🍴M**P**24a, 24b; photographs page 110). The monastery, steeped in legend and history, was founded in the 8th century, when a small chapel was built. The present buildings date from the 17th and 18th centuries. The church, built between 1622 and 1724, was considerably altered at the beginning of the 1900s. It is an important Catholic sanctuary; visitors come here from all over the island, and pilgrimages are often made on foot up to the monastery. The museum contains coin collections, typical dress, and items of archaeological merit. Also of great interest is the Ca S'Amitger, just by the entrance to the car park, with its colourful, illuminated photographs of

Roman bridge at Pollença

Mallorca's flora and fauna, including many varieties of indigenous orchids. Here you will get an insight into the life of the great black vulture — the island, and Europe's, largest bird of prey. Of most importance to countryside

lovers, however, is the opportunity to stay overnight at Lluc — the best base for many superb mountain hikes (Walks 12, 22 and 24-26 among them). So, there's plenty to keep you busy here, until supper at one of the three local restaurants and a peaceful night's sleep in the heart of the mountains!

Day two: After breakfast at the monastery, rejoin the Ma-10 in direction of Pollença. Pass the entrance to Binifaldó (83.5km **P**24d) — Walks 24 and 25 come this way — and then some excellent woodland picnic sites (84km ⊞**P**26). Walk 26 begins here, following the old route to Pollença. The narrow road snakes through a dramatic rocky landscape of high mountains and valleys, passing the entrance to Mortitx at KM10.9. Walk 27 starts and ends here; it leads through a 'wild-west' landscape to the coastal cliffs shown on page 121. Now the road winds down toward the northern tip of the island, with magnificent views over Pollença's bay.

Ascending Ses Voltes, on the climb to Galileu (Walk 12 from Lluc)

Come into **Pollença★** (100km ⊹▲✕☎⊕M); just by the first turning into this market-garden town, the Roman bridge★ shown opposite (⋔) — the only original one left on Mallorca, still stands over the Torrent de Sant Jordi. Behind the main square the cypress-bordered stone stairway shown on page 120 (right) leads up to a tiny 18th-century chapel atop Calvary Hill★, from where an impressive view of the bay can be enjoyed; there are 365 steps up, one for each day of the year — a good leg-stretcher! Opposite the town one can see the Puig de Maria★ (333m/1090ft); a 45min walk to the top would take you to a hermitage with more stunning panoramic views of both Pollença and Alcúdia's bays. (You could stay overnight at the monastery, with its restaurant and bar, at nominal cost.)

Leaving Pollença, continue towards the sea along the Ma-2200, passing the turn-off to Cala Sant Vicenç (▲✕) at 102km and coming into **Port de Pollença★** (106km ▲✕ ☎⊕M), a touristic but tranquil resort ensconced at the northern end of Pollença Bay. To visit, keep ahead at both roundabouts to the seafront, where you can park by the marina (just round to the right). Walk along the beautiful traffic-free esplanade (left), where a multitude of bright parasols shade the seafront cafés, and white yachts bob up and down on a deep blue sea at the marina. Or follow Walk 28 up into the Bóquer Valley (P28; photograph page 15), a bird-watchers' paradise hidden between the craggy peaks of the Cavall Bernat and the Bóquer Ridge.

To continue, return to the first roundabout out of the port, and go right on the ring road behind the port, signposted to Formentor (Ma-2200Å). Walk 28 turns off left at the third roundabout along this road. Once beyond Port de Pollença, start to wind uphill, negotiating several sharp bends. You soon arrive at the splendidly-engineered **Mirador d'es Colomer★** (113km 🎦), where stone steps skirt the edge of a high rock cliff and end at a precipitous viewpoint hundreds of feet above the sea — definitely the best place to photograph the Formentor headland and Es Colomer ('Pigeon Rock'). Opposite this viewpoint, a narrow tarmac lane winds up to a 16th-century watchtower, the Talaia de Albercutx, with unsurpassed views of the Formentor and Pollença bays, but I recommend you walk up, not drive, as there is very little room to turn around at the top.

The tour continues over the pass, and winds down between pine woods towards the magnificent bay, where pale turquoise and aquamarine waters lap onto white sands. Ahead lies the famous Hotel Formentor, above an idyllic stretch of white sandy beach. Its opening in 1926 was heralded by illuminated advertisements in Paris, hence it became — and still is — a favourite paradise by the sea

for the 'jet-set', politicians, and film stars. Continuing left, a winding road over the rocky headland (with two more *miradors*) will bring you to the northernmost tip, the **Cap de Formentor★** (128km 🎦) and its lighthouse, perched high on the jagged cliff-tops — the home of Eleonora's falcons. From here an exciting 15-minutes descent on the steps of the 'Itinerario del Moll del Patronat' drops you down 100m, almost to sea level, to a disused landing jetty — a perfect leg-stretcher before starting the return drive along this headland.

Leaving the unique beauty of the Formentor cape, return to Port de Pollença and, back on the seafront (Ma-2200), go right to drive round the bay beside the sea. At the roundabout at the far end, go left to come into **Alcúdia★** (158km 🛉✕🍴 and **M** of Roman antiquities), the capital city of Mallorca during Roman times. Originally named 'Pollentia', the thriving city flourished from the 2nd century BC until the 6th century, when it was destroyed by invading Vandals. Parts of the old city wall still remain, rebuilt during the reign of Jaime II, by which time the town had been renamed Alcúdia (derived from a Moorish word for 'hill'). The Roman amphitheatre is worth a visit.

At the second set of traffic lights, continue ahead, following signposts to Mal Pas, to drive along the headland towards the Cape of Pines. At the junction by the Bodega del Sol bar in **Mal Pas**, a road left leads to two beautiful sandy beaches that most tourists miss and, off to the right, a narrow lane leads to Victoria Park (P29c), where Walk 29 ends. But for the moment keep ahead down to the sea. Turn right past Crocodile Port, drive up the hill and then wind down to cross a small bridge. Continue along this beautiful stretch of coastal road between the pines (164km ✕⊓). Passing a junction, keep ahead towards the cape, for some splendid photography at the **Cap d'es Pinar**★ headland (165km 📷). The road ends here at a tunnel in the rock, just above the picturesque sandy coves of Ses Caletes, with spectacular views back across the bay to the Formentor Cape.

Return to the junction, and go up left, to climb in sharp bends to the **Ermita de la Victoria**★ (166.5km ⬆⊓📷*P*29a, 29b; photograph page 126), where Walk 29 begins and Walk 30 begins and ends. Visit the old church and the viewpoint (walk down some steps to the left of the church and go straight along a narrow path). There is overnight accommodation in the small and elegant Hostatgería above the church, with fabulous views across the bay. And the restaurant here must have one of the most privileged positions on the island; its terrace overlooks the wide bay — a wonderful place to dine on a summer evening, when the lights of the port twinkle over the dark bay.

Return to the traffic lights and turn left. Go right at the first roundabout (the Ma-3460), then left at the second (signposted 'Artà') and left at the third. This brings you into **Port d'Alcúdia** (175km 🏖✕⊕), famous for the freshly-caught lobsters and other seafoods available in most of the beach-side restaurants. Further along is the commercial port, where ferries to Menorca and France dock in the deep harbour. You can park on any of the back streets behind the beautiful tiled promenade and wide sandy beach.

To continue, return to the round-about and go left towards Artà along the Ma-12. The road runs past luxury hotels, villas, holiday apartments and shops bordering one of the longest and most beautiful stretches of white sandy beach and dunes on the island. After a straight run of almost 3km, at the second set of traffic lights (180km), turn right, following the sign to 'Sa Pobla'. This narrow road (Ma-3431) borders the marshlands of S'Albufera (Car tour 4), passing by Alcúdia's electricity station and then through farmlands, to **Sa Pobla** (✕⊕), an agricultural town benefitting from extremely fertile soil. From here fruit and vegetables, especially potatoes, are exported all over Europe. Keep ahead through the town, and then turn right on the Ma-3430, following signs to Palma. Further on, go round to the right, and then left on the Ma-3420, and straight ahead at the roundabouts. You emerge on the Ma-13A, where you go left over the flyover, towards Palma.

One final visit is a 'must', however, before you return to the capital: at the next junction, turn right, to follow narrow country lanes signposted to the **Coves de Campanet**★ (197km). These fabulous underground halls are resplendent with dramatically-lighted stalactites and stalagmites, and cannot be missed! Then maybe enjoy a drink on the terrace before returning to the Ma-13A. A straight run along this road (ample 🅿) would take you back to Palma after 235km.

If you're running late, pick up the motorway. Alternatively, if you have time in hand, consider taking a detour from **Inca**, via Lloseta (where Walk 15 ends) to Alaró and the beautiful Orient Valley (*P*14; photograph page 92), where Walks 14 and 15 begin.

4 VILLAGES OFF THE BEATEN TRACK AND THE 'FAR EAST'

Palma • Natura Parc • Sineu • Maria de la Salut • Santa Margalida • Ca'n Picafort • S'Albufera • Colònia de Sant Pere • Artà • Cala Ratjada • Capdepera • Coves d'Artà • Sant Llorenç • Manacor • Petra • Sant Joan • Algaida • Palma

231km/143mi; 6h driving
On route: ☐ at the Natura Parc, S'Albufera; Picnics (see pages 10-15): (7, 8, 31); Walks: (7, 8, 31)
Opening hours/market days
The **Natura Parc** (tel: 971-144078) is open from 10.00-19.00 (summer), 10.00-18.00 (winter); closed 25/12 and 1/1. The reception area for the **S'Albufera** marshlands (tel: 971-892250) is open from 09.00-13.00 and 14.00-17.00 in winter and 14.00-19.00 in summer. The **Museo Arqueológico** at Artà opens daily from 10.00-18.00.

The **Coves d'Artà** (Caves; tel: 971-841293) are open daily from 10.00-18.00 (summer) and 10.00-17.00 (winter), guided visit every half hour.
Markets — Sineu: Wednesday mornings; **Maria de la Salut:** Friday mornings; **Santa Margalida:** Tuesday and Saturday mornings; **Ca'n Picafort:** Tuesday afternoons; **Artà:** Tuesday mornings; **Sant Llorenç:** Thursday mornings; **Manacor:** Monday mornings; **Petra:** Wednesday mornings; **Algaida:** Friday mornings

I t's best to start out early if you want to complete this tour in one day, otherwise it is an ideal two-day programme, allowing more time for visits. Most of the roads are in good condition, although between Petra and Algaida we travel on little-used country lanes. At time of writing, the Manacor road (Ma-15) is being widened.

Leave Palma either from the 'Avenidas' or the ring road ('Via Cintura') by taking the Manacor exit off the roundabout (Ma-15). Keep ahead on this wide road, and at the first roundabout go left on the Ma-3018, signposted to 'Camí Salard'. At the next roundabout, go right on the Ma-3011, signposted to Sineu, to drive out of Palma and into the countryside (✗ at 5.5km). After winding up over a low hill, turn right opposite a petrol station and a large sign to **Natura Parc★** (16km ✗🍴). This is a wonderful place to begin today's tour, especially for children and, of course, animal lovers. You can take morning coffee at the rest area, before or after seeing all kinds of animals — llamas, deer, roe, ostriches, vultures, marabous, and other exotic creatures. Don't

miss the butterfly garden, with over 500 species.
Back on the Ma-3011, at 17.5km pass the turn-off to Santa Eugènia (*P*7, 8; Walks 7, 8), and continue through open countryside along this wide but tranquil route, once a Roman road; it heads in an almost straight line towards the centre of the island.
Come into the agricultural village of **Sineu** (33km 🏚️✝️✗🍴), but do *not* follow signs to the right. Keep on to the end, and at the 'Stop' sign go left, following signs to 'Totes direccions' (All directions), skirting the lower end of the village. At the next 'Stop' sign (where there is 🍴 100m down to the left, should you need it), again go straight on to the end, then follow the road round to the right, now parallel with the railway lines.

30

S'Albufera

Ignore the first turning left to 'Llubì' and, when you come to a third 'Stop' sign, turn left for 'María de la Salut' to continue the tour. (But to visit Sineu's Wednesday market, go straight on to a car park by the station.) Sineu, named Sixneu in Arabic times and Sinium by the Romans, holds a lively agricultural market on Wednesday mornings, a tradition kept from as far back as the Middle Ages — this market has been held weekly for over 800 years! Nowadays, not only will you find animals and stalls piled high with fresh vegetables and fruit, but almost anything that can be sold, from delicate porcelains to hand-embroidered shawls, copper pots, leatherware, shoes, etc. The ambience is one of rural charm, and people visit from all over the island. To continue, turn left towards 'María' and, just after a windmill and restaurant, at the roundabout, cross the wide road, taking the Ma-3510 opposite towards Maria.

This pleasant bucolic run over undulating countryside (📷 at 35.5km) makes a change from the mountainous routes followed in previous tours. Soon you come to a small country village, **Maria de la Salut** (38km 📷♦✕⊕), far from the whirlwinds of coastal tourism. These lands once belonged to the infamous Ramón Zaforteza, whose cruelty earned him the name 'Evil Count'. The local church has an interesting baroque bell tower. On entering the village, take the first left and then go right, following signs to 'Santa Margalida' (Margarita) and coming onto the Ma-3520 and out once more into rolling countryside. At the next junction, turn left on the Ma-3340, to come to **Santa Margalida** (42.5km ♦), an ancient settlement inhabited both by Romans and Arabs, set on a low rise with excellent views of the

distant sierra. At the roundabout, keep right, following signs to Ca'n Picafort along the Ma-3410. Coming over the top of the rise, you now have wonderful views of the wide bay of Alcúdia, with the Cap de Menorca on the left horizon and the Artà mountains off to the right. At the next junction keep straight ahead (in spite of the sign to 'Ca'n Picafort' pointing right). After a long straight stretch come into **Ca'n Picafort** (52.5km 📷△✕🛒⊕), where a long wide beach stretches out, bordered by miles of sand dunes, and a tiled esplanade shaded by many multi-coloured sun umbrellas offers the choice of countless sea-front cafés. To visit the **Albufera** marshlands (a 'must' for nature-lovers, go left at the roundabout and follow the Ma-12 as far as a little bridge (Es Pont dels Anglesos); the entrance is off to the left just before the bridge. It's about 1km along the lane to the reception area — either drive or walk to it; entrance is free. Many footpaths cross the reeded marshes, with several 'hides' at strategic points — a bird-watchers' paradise! Some of the resident marsh-dwellers you might see are crakes, terns, warblers or hoopoes, and sandpipers, as well as egrets or wagtails in winter, together with migrating herons or cranes. Kestrels, ospreys and marsh harriers also abound, as do many others. There are orchids here, too, and a multitude of colourful wild flowers in spring. Near the reception, there's an interesting

31

museum with audiovisual effects.
Back in Ca'n Picafort (where a left
at the roundabout leads to the sea-
front), keep along the Ma-12 to
the far end of the resort. Then go
left at the roundabout, following
signs to 'Son Baulo'. Take the next
right and, at the end of this road
turn right; park by the Hotel Son
Baulo, and walk onto the beach,
by a beautiful lagoon. Bearing
right along this wide beach, over
the sand dunes, you will come to
one of the most important
prehistoric settlements of the
Balearics, the **Son Real Necro-
polis**; it is well-preserved and
worth seeing.
Back in your car, follow this same
road round in a circle and turn up
left, back to the roundabout on the
Ma-12. Go left now, towards Artà,
along a wide country road. You
pass turn-offs right to Santa Margarita (63km), left to Son Serra de
la Marina (64km; a characterless
waterfront mass of chalets), and
right to Petra (67km ☎) and
Manacor (69km). At 70km turn
left on the Ma-3331, soon coming
to the turn-off left down to
Colònia de Sant Pere (75km
▲▲△✕), the last little enclave on
the eastern side of Alcúdia bay.
This is a sweet little resort with a
stretch of colourful cafés and
awnings above the small beach,
yachts bobbing up and down in
the sheltered harbour, and extensive views across the wide bay as
far as the distant Formentor headland (Car tour 3).
Back on the Ma-3331, go left for
Betlem, a residential area set on
the rocks, with the stark backdrop

of the Artà range reflecting in the
deep blue waters. (At 79.5km a
signposted footpath rises in 50
minutes to the Ermita de Betlem,
which we visit later in this tour.)
After a roundabout, you come to
the 'Fishermen's Village' (80.5km
✕). Past here the tarmac ends, but
a sandy track goes on for a couple
of kilometres — a beautiful coastal
walk through pine woods, ending
at a rocky cove; there is also a
rocky trail down to two hidden
beaches near the start of the
track.
Returning to the Ma-12, turn left
to continue over a mountainous
landscape to **Artà** (96km
✝▲✕☎⊕M). There is quite a lot
to see here, so you will need to
spend some time. On entering the
town, keep straight ahead,
following signs to the 'Ermita',
then keeping left in the square. Go
straight ahead at all junctions and,
at the top of the narrow street,
turn right. Then take the second
left, signposted 'Ermita de
Betlem'. Rise past the high wall of
the Almudaina to leave the town,
winding away up into the hills
again (99km ▲▲✕) for some 9km
(the last 4km are narrow and
winding). An access road to
Aubarca and Es Verger, a protected wilderness area of mountains and valleys reaching down to
the virgin coasts of the Artà
mountains, is well signposted not
far past the KM5 marker. (On
Walk 31 this area is approached on
foot from Cala Estreta, to the
east.)
You arrive at **S'Ermita de Betlem**
(107km ✝☎), a sanctuary set on a
mountaintop in the middle of
nowhere. Here a silent cypress-
lined avenue leads up to the
hermitage, instilling peace into the
soul. To find the best viewpoint,
go to the left of the building and

through the small gate at the back, to follow a stony trail over the brow of the mountain for stunning views down over the wide bay of Alcúdia and the distant rocky Formentor Peninsula, with the Colònia de Sant Pere and Betlem below on the coast. Just below the gates, a track leads down to a mountain spring under the rocks, a nice picnic spot. These mountains were once the private shooting grounds of the ancient kings of Mallorca.

Back in Artà, keep left up to the top of the hill to visit the Almudaina, the site of a Moorish fortress, where the **Santuari de Sant Salvador** still stands. You can walk round the parapets to admire the town from above. The archeological museum is also worth a visit; it contains many important pieces, including five bronze statuettes dating from the 2nd century BC. Finally, you won't want to miss a nearby prehistoric village: to get there, descend from the Almudaina and the church and turn left, following Carrer Major all the way to the end. When you meet the Ma-15 on the far side of town (116km), turn left; some 100m along, on a bend, lies the entrance to **Ses Paisses**★ (117km 🏛), where you can see the *talaiots* (stone structures) of an ancient civilisation.

Return to the Ma-15 and turn right towards Cala Ratjada, passing the turn off left to Cala Estreta (*P*31 and Walk 31; photographs page 128) about 1km out of town. On approaching Capdepera, where a medieval fortress with parapets crowns the top of the hill, go left at the roundabout, skirting the village, and left again at the next roundabout. Come into **Cala Ratjada** (128km 🛥️🍴🚉⊕), a picturesque fishing port on the easternmost tip of the island. To

get to the beach (Cala Agulla) keep left; for the port go right. It's definitely worth driving up the twisting road from the port to the lighthouse (130.5km 📷) for the views. Return towards the port and, at the bottom of the lighthouse road, turn left to **Cala Gat** (131.5km), a beautiful blue cove in a rocky recess, lovely for swimming.

Leave Cala Ratjada by following signs through the one-way system back to the roundabout, and go straight on to **Capdepera** (134km ✝🏛🍴⊕); here you can walk around the parapets for panoramic views over Cala Ratjada and the pine-wooded coast, or visit the small oratory inside the wall built by King Sancho during the 14th century. To visit, turn right where you see the sign to 'Castell'.

From Capdepera follow signs to Canyamel along the Ma-4040. Some 1.5km after the last roundabout, turn left towards 'Coves d'Artà' (caves), and after a long straight run, go left again on the Ma-4042. This winds up to the **Coves d'Artà** ★ (142km 📷). An impressive stone stairway leads you into a huge black hole under the cliff; your journey into these fantastic underground halls, once the hideout of pirates, has begun. It will take you through an unreal landscape of thousands of cleverly-lit stalactites and stalagmites, and eerie caverns of imposing grandeur.

After this impressive visit, and once your eyes have readjusted to the daylight, return down the road past a viewpoint down over Canyamel beach, your next destination (📷 at 143km). Further on, veer left at the junction signposted to Artà and Palma. Shortly, turn left towards the **Torre de Canyamel** (148km 🍴; photograph and notes page 56). Further along, go left at the roundabout, to come to the

Platja de Canyamel (152km ▲✕), a beautiful wide sandy bay, bordered on either side by high pine-covered cliffs.

Doubling back on your tracks, return to the junction and keep straight ahead towards Artà, then go left at the roundabout back onto the Ma-4040. After the tunnel, a straight run takes you to **Son Servera** (163km ⚲🚐⊕). Keep straight ahead at the roundabout, skirting the village, to join onto the Ma-4030 for another straight run into **Sant Llorenç d'es Cardassar** (169.5km ⚲✕🚐⊕), an agricultural village. When you meet the Ma-15, turn left.

From here it's about 6km (🚐 at 171.5km, ✕ at 172km) to **Manacor** (176km ⚲▲✕🚐⊕M), the second largest town on Mallorca, mostly industrial. It is the centre for hand-carved furniture, and there are good ceramic shops — as well as the world-famous 'Majorica' pearl factory, visited daily by coachloads of tourists. In 1229, when Jaime I took Manacor back from the Moors, there was even a mosque and several noble Arab dwellings in this town.

Leave Manacor along the Ma-15, and at 180km go right on the Ma-3320 signposted to Petra, a busy wide route across the centre of the island. At the first roundabout go left into **Petra** (187.5km ⚲🚐⊕M), birthplace of Fray Juniper Serra, the Franciscan monk who founded many missions in North America — some of which later became great cities such as San Diego and San Francisco (there is a bust commemorating this in Washington DC). It is a little difficult to find his house of birth (with museum) in the labyrinth of narrow streets: keep to the end of the road and then turn right, following the signs to 'Sant Joan'; pass a church and then go left, now signposted 'Birthplace of Fray Juniper Serra'. The house is further along, up a narrow cobbled 'no-entry' street — parking is difficult, so it is better to park near the church and go on foot.

Your homeward route now leaves Petra along an as-yet unspoilt old country lane (Ma-3220, signposted to Sant Joan), crossing a lonely landscape of agricultural fields and low hills, eventually coming to **Sant Joan** (196km ✕⊕), where a popular *romería* is celebrated just before Easter, the 'Festival of Bread and Fishes', and the local housewives bake homemade fish pasties. Do *not* follow the signs to Palma, but turn up right, and then go left, following the signs to Pina. At the junction outside Sant Joan keep straight ahead along the Ma-3230. Driving into the sunset, you now follow this winding country lane over an undulating and peaceful landscape, thus avoiding the busy Ma-15 for a little longer. At the next junction, keep left towards Algaida (signposted).

At 210km pick up the Ma-15 at the roundabout on the outskirts of **Algaida** (⚲✕🚐⊕), for a straight run (ample ✕🚐) back to Palma's ring road (231km).

Ses Paisses

5 THE ROUTE OF CAVES AND MONASTERIES

Palma • Manacor • Coves dels Hams • Reserva Africana • Porto Cristo • Coves del Drac • Calas de Mallorca • Porto Colom • Santuari de Sant Salvador • Felanitx • Castell de Santueri • Cala d'Or • Porto Petro • Santanyí • Cala Figuera • Ses Salines • Colònia de Sant Jordi • Campos • Santuari de Monti-Sion • Porreres • Palma

252km/156mi; 6h driving (a two-day tour)

On route: 🍴 at the Coves dels Hams, Coves del Drac and Santuari de Sant Salvador

Opening hours/market days

The **Santuari de Sant Salvador** (tel: 971-827282) is open daily; beautiful, economical new hostelry with stunning views, or stay in the monastery itself.

The **Coves dels Hams** (Caves; tel: 971-820988) are open daily from 10.00-13.30 and 14.00-17.30 in winter, 10.30-13.00 and 14.00-18.00 in summer; there is a tour (with concert) every 20 minutes.

The **Reserva Africana** (safari park; tel: 971 810909) is open daily from 10.00-16.00 in winter and from 09.00-19.00 in summer.

The **Coves del Drac** (Caves; tel: 971-820753) are open daily from 10.00-17.00; hourly concerts from 10:45-16:30 (15.00 in winter).

The **Acuario de Mallorca** opens daily from 11.00-15.00 in winter, from 10.30-18.00 in summer.

Markets — Manacor: Monday mornings; **Felanitx:** Sunday mornings; **Santanyí:** Saturday mornings; **Colònia de Sant Jordi:** Wednesday mornings; **Campos:** Thursday mornings; **Porreres:** Tuesday mornings; **Montuïri:** Monday mornings

Y ou *could* do this tour in one day, but to do justice to all the sights (the caves are one of the natural wonders of the world), I suggest a two-day programme. Spend the night at a mountaintop monastery, where monks straight out of the Middle Ages, with long white beards and wearing brown hooded robes, glide silently between the sanctuary walls; it is quite an experience. At time of writing, the Manacor road (Ma-15) is being widened.

Leave Palma either from the 'Avenidas' or the ring road ('Via Cintura') by taking the Manacor exit off the roundabout. Following the Ma-15 through beautiful open countryside, you bypass Algaida (19km ♦✕☕⊕), Montuïri (26.5km ✕⊕) and Vilafranca de Bonany (35.5km ✕☕⊕). More rolling green hills accompany you to the island's second largest town, **Manacor** (46km ♦▲✕☕⊕M; see Car tour 4). Keep straight on into the town, then turn right at the second traffic lights (48km) towards 'Porto Cristo', following the same signs through the town's wide palm-lined avenues.

Out in the country again, follow the Ma-4020 (✕ at 51km, ☕ at

53km). At 59km (✕) turn right along the tree-lined entrance to the **Coves dels Hams★**. Stretch your legs on a visit to these magnificent subterranean hallways and underground lakes, discovered only in the early 1900s by a Mallorcan speleologist. Have morning coffee at the open-air café.

Back on the road, turn right for Porto Cristo, and on entering the town (visited later in the tour), go left at the roundabout, following signs to Son Servera. You come onto the Ma-4023 — the road to the safari park (several ✕). Pass by the turn-offs to Cala Moreia and S'Illot, and turn left at the signpost 'Safari', coming to the **Reserva Africana★** (66km ☕). This is an

35

auto-safari, and you can either drive your own car or take the little train; it's a real thrill to see so many animals — rhinos, elephants, ostriches, giraffes, hippos, monkeys, crocodiles and many, many more. The children will love it.

After this exciting 'memory of Africa', return to **Porto Cristo** (71.5km ▲▲ ✕), thought to be an important sea port in Roman times. Keep straight on at the roundabouts, then go right down a steep hill (signposted 'Coves del Drac'), coming to the picturesque fishing port and beach. There is quite a good parking area down left below the small esplanade, if you wish to explore. There are also boat trips from the jetty.

Continuing, follow the 'Cuevas del Drach' signposting, and go left at an oval roundabout, to reach the **Coves del Drac★** (73.5km ✕) just outside the port. The Arch-duke Luis Salvador of Austria (see pages 22-23 and 80) discovered these caves on his extensive travels on Mallorca and commissioned the French geologist, Martel, to explore them and and map them out. The hour-long guided tour takes you through a labyrinth of stone corridors, steps, and brilliantly-illuminated caverns, and ends with the mystical strains of violins drifting across the still waters of an underground lake reflecting a thousand stalactites… a floating concert. Nearby, the **Acuario de Mallorca** makes another colourful and fascinating visit, where you'll see exotic fish from the Australian coral reef, dreaded piranhas from Brazil, and Mediterranean sharks.

Return to the main road and go left at the oval roundabout towards 'Calas de Mallorca' along the Ma-4014, a country lane that runs parallel with the coast through almond orchards and open fields. At 79km, pass the turn-off to Cala Romántica (✕) — another pretty cove. At 83km, on a sharp bend, go left on a rough tarmac road, eventually arriving at the unprepossesing **Calas de Mallorca** (86km ▲▲ ✕) — just a clump of ugly hotels sitting ostentatiously on the rocks. However, the best 'view' can be had by turning left at the sign to the Hotel Sol Canarios and driving down the dirt track to the point where it bends down right towards the cove. Here you can walk over the rocky headland to the left, to find an untouched part of the coastline, even though the opposite side of the main *cala* is totally overbuilt.

Back on the road, go left just by the Hotel Sol Canarios and, after the bend, you will see a road off right, signposted to Cala Murada. Follow this road out of the Calas, rising and dropping sharply over the hills; it's just like being on the big dipper! Pass the turn-off to Cala Domingos (88km) and when you come to the 'Stop' sign, go left. Keep down the main road, ignoring all signs to 'Círculo'. At the fork, go right, to come to small bay of **Cala Murada** (94km ▲▲ ✕), also blighted by development, although the sandy cove is quite pleasant.

Return along the same road, continuing straight ahead at the junction. When you rejoin the Ma-4014, turn left. At the end, go left again on the Ma-4010 (✕), to come to **Porto Colom** (103km ▲▲ ✕), a centuries-old commercial and fishing port, now also a residential area and summer resort popular among the Mallorcans. From the roundabout at the entrance you can keep straight ahead to visit the seafront, go right to Cala Marçal, or go left on the Ma-4060, signposted 'Far' (light-house). The lighthouse road, a

narrow tarmac lane, rounds the port, with picturesque views of fishing schooners and boat-houses, and climbs to the lighthouse on the headland, with panoramic views over the port (🖭).
Return to the Ma-4010 and head towards Felanitx, but turn left just before the town (114km; signposted 'Santuari de Sant Salvador'). This winding road climbs the steep slopes to the **Santuari de Sant Salvador★** (128km 🛉🛏✕🎋🖭) at a height of 510m/1675ft, with impressive panoramas. An enormous monument (37m/120ft high) dominates the car park. A short walk takes you up to the monastery buildings, where a valuable Gothic altarpiece can be seen encased in glass. Enquiries for your overnight stay can be made either inside the terrace bar, where a beautiful hostelry has opened (rooms with stunning views) or inside the monastery itself at the souvenir shop. Imagine waking up to these panoramic views with tomorrow's rising sun!
Day two: Leave the monastery, wind back down to the Ma4010, and turn left to come into **Felanitx** (125km 🛉🛏✕🖳⊕), a wine-making town, also famous for its ceramics. Its church is built from the same honey-coloured stone as Palma's cathedral. Follow signs to Palma, going right at the first roundabout and left at the second, along palm-lined avenues. Drive through the town guided by the 'Santyí' signs. After passing the tree-shaded square, turn right on the Ma-14, at first heading left. Then follow the one-way system: second left; right up to the top of the rise; left again to regain the Ma-14, the 'Carrer de Santueri'. Turn right, uphill, and leave the town. About 1.5km along, turn left on a narrow country lane signposted 'Castell', winding into the low hills past orchards, orange

groves and vineyards, then climbing steeply to the **Castell de Santueri★** (135km ▪🖭). This castle was reconstructed over the remains of a Moorish stronghold during the 13th century, a very strategic position. In summer, the door is open and on payment of a small fee, you can walk around the remaining fortress walls, with stunning views on all sides.
Return to the Ma-14 and go left towards 'Santanyí'. At the next junction (142.5km) go left again on the Ma-4016 towards 'Cala d'Or', passing through the hamlet of **Es Carritxò**, and then winding up and down between the hills. At the roundabout, go right on the Ma-4012. Coming into **Calonge** (148km 🛉✕), take the first left; after a long straight stretch you reach **Cala d'Or** (151km 🛏✕🖳⊕). This dazzling-white summer resort straddles aquamarine and turquoise-hued coves, where sandy beaches hide. Visit the marina, where expensive yachts and fishing boats bob up and down on the deep blue sea, or take refreshments at one of the waterside cafés.
From Cala d'Or follow signs to Porto Petro along the ring road behind the resort, going right at a roundabout (153.5km). Wind down into **Porto Petro** (154km 🛉🛏✕), another attractive little harbour. Drive round the scenic inlet and then go right on the wide Ma-19A signposted to Santanyí and Palma. At **Alquería Blanca** (160km 🛉✕), keep straight up the main road, out into the country again, still on the Ma-19A. You pass the turn-off right up to the Ermita de la Consolación (162km), a small 17th-century oratory, and soon after you arrive at **Santanyí** (167km 🛉✕🖳⊕). Go right here, following signs to Cala Figuera along the ring road, keeping ahead at the roundabouts.

At the T-junction (169.5km), go right on the Ma-6102 for a straight run to **Cala Figuera** (173km 🏖🍴). Scene of many an onslaught by pirates and Saracens in the past, it must surely be one of the prettiest *calas* in Mallorca. Drive down to the 'Port', and park on the slope; the rest of the way is pedestrianised. Picturesque views over fishing boats moored in the cove can be enjoyed by continuing uphill on foot, or stretch your legs along the rocky headland.

Back on the Ma-6102, you can visit the beautiful beach of Cala Santanyí by turning left (signposted) some 700m out of Cala Figuera; follow the road through the residential zone and, at the 'Stop' sign, go left down the slope to **Cala Santanyí** (175.5km 🏖🍴). Drive straight ahead, past the car park and beach, out of the bay, and go right at the junction. Back on the Ma-6102, turn left to return to **Santanyí**. On entering the town, take the first left towards 'Cala Llombards', then go left again at the roundabout (same signposting), to drive out of town on the Ma-6100. Soon you pass the left turn to Cala Llombards (and Cala S'Almonia, a picturesque fishing village set on the rocks, with an enormous blowhole). Drive through the village of **Es Llombards** (181km 🍴) and, still on the Ma-6100, follow signs to Ses Salines, passing the left turn to Cap Salines, on the southernmost tip of the island.

Ses Salines (184km 🍴📮⊕) is an agricultural village near the salt flats (hence its name). There are remains of several prehistoric talayotic settlements here, as well as Roman tombs scattered about from here as far as the coast. Go through the village, bearing left at both roundabouts, towards 'Colònia Sant Jordi'. Pass a left turn to a prehistoric site (185.5km) and,

still on the Ma-6100, continue straight into **Colònia de Sant Jordi** (191km 🏖🍴📮⊕). Go straight over the roundabout, past the petrol station, and on to a square. Then park on one of the side streets and walk on to the port. Boats leave here for the isle of Cabrera in summer (a sometimes choppy crossing). Apart from the seafront restaurants, the real attractions here are the long white sandy beaches further round the bay.

Return to the roundabout and go left towards Palma and Campos. At a roundabout (197.5km) go straight ahead towards Campos, a town dating from the 1300s. No less than five watchtowers were built in Campos during the 14th century! The church boasts an original painting by the Spanish artist, Murillo, which usually hung in the Sant Blai hermitage nearby. Apart from this, Campos is basically an agricultural centre and does not have a great deal to offer the tourist. Go left once in **Campos** (204km 🚻🍴📮⊕), and then right, past the petrol station; follow signs to Porreres through Campos, coming out onto the Ma-5040 for a pleasant country run. At a pink signpost for 'Monti-Sion' go left on the Ma-5030 (212.5km); go left again 1km further on (same pink signpost), to climb a low hill up to the **Santuari de Monti-Sion** (215km 🚻🏛🍴📷). Admire the far-reaching views down over the fertile plain, before climbing the steps to enter the peaceful courtyard with its Gothic-style stone archways and central well.

Back down on the Ma-5030, go left towards Montuïri, bypassing Porreres and soon coming to a roundabout on the Ma-15 just by Montuïri (224km). Go left for a straight run (ample 🍴📮) back to Palma's ring road (252km.).

6 SOUTHERN RESORTS AND THE PUIG DE RANDA

Palma • Es Molinar • Coll d'en Rabassa • Ca'n Pastilla • S'Arenal • Cap Blanc • Cala Pí • Capocorp Vell • S'Estanyol • Ses Covetes and Es Trenc • Campos • Llucmajor • Puig de Randa and Santuari de Cura • Palma

136km/84mi; 4h driving
On route: ⊓ at the Santuari de Cura; Picnic 32 (page 15); Walk 32
Opening hours/market days
Capocorp Vell (megalithic village; tel: 971 180155) is open from 10.00-17.00; closed Thursdays
Markets — Campos: Thursday mornings; **Llucmajor:** Wednesday and Sunday mornings

Although there is less of touristic interest on this car tour, it is ideal for the summer, as it leads to several beautiful beaches. We end up at the Puig de Randa, from where the whole of our itinerary is captured in a magnificent view over the coast.

Leave Palma from the eastern end of the 'Avenidas', going left towards 'Platja de Palma', and turn off right at the traffic light (0.7km ✕) to **Es Molinar**. The road rounds a charming little fishing port, and at the end you can turn right for the sea-front. Here, overlooking Palma Bay, is the famous Portixol restaurant, popular for its wonderful fresh seafood dishes. You can only drive a little way along the front, past 'old world'-style terraced houses, then must head back onto the main road (🚱 at 2.5km). There are also some very good seafood restaurants at **Coll d'en Rabassa** (4km ⌂⌂ ✕) — and the lovely wide sandy beach of Ciutat Jardí ('City Garden'), mostly visited by Palma city-dwellers. Back on the main road, continue up through the shopping area and, at the last set of traffic lights (4.5km), turn right (signposted to Ca'n Pastilla). Soon after passing the electricity plant, you come into **Ca'n Pastilla** (6km ⌂⌂ ✕ 🚱 ⊕). The tourist resort begins here and, edged by miles of wide sandy beach, stretches out all the way to S'Arenal, with plenty of shops to browse through and a myriad of sea-front cafés.

At the end of Ca'n Pastilla, turn left, then right, to continue on the long road (🚱 at 7.5km) that runs behind a string of hotels, restaurants, barbecue stalls and holiday blocks (as the main part of the sea-front has been pedestrianised). However, towards the end of **S'Arenal** (12.5km ⌂⌂ ✕ 🚱 ⊕), you can turn right down any of the side streets, to come to the beach,

Ses Covetes

then continue along the front all the way to the end. Then go up the steepish slope of the Carrer Sant Bartolomé (signposted 'Cala Blava'). At the top, keep right, along the middle of the three roads, past more hotels. At the roundabout, go right again along the Ma-6014 towards Cala Blava. This road escapes into the country-side (🅿 at 15.5km). Keep left at the next roundabout, along the Ma-6014, across a rather desolate landscape of low scrub, where various new residential zones pop up sporadically like oases in a desert along this vast stretch of arid bushland.

An interesting detour, with a breathtaking view of the coastline and cliffs, comes up at the residential zone called 'Los Delfines' (22km): turn right where you see the dolphin statues, down Jupiter Street, and then turn down left along Carrer Creu del Sud. Drive all the way to the end, then go halfway round the small round-about. Now go sharp right down what appears to be the entrance to a house, and drive down a cobbled road (📷), zigzagging down the cliff to a wide car park. If you've time, and the weather's good, descend the wooden steps to sea level to swim off the rocks.

Back up on the Ma-6014, go right to continue along the cliff-top road, coming to the lighthouse at **Cap Blanc** (33km 📷; photograph page 129), the 'White Cape'. Both the lighthouse and the 16th-century watchtower at the left of the point are now fenced off, although you might like to stop for photographs.

From Cap Blanc the road swings inland and heads once more into open country. At 39km turn off right towards Cala Pí. A rough narrow road takes you across miles of dry scrubland to the beautiful creek of **Cala Pí** (42km ⛰✕;

photograph page 130), where a lovely beach hides between the cliffs. Drive to the end of the road, and park by or near the watch-tower, from where you can see the magical Isle of Cabrera on the blue horizon. Then walk back to find the steps down to the creek. Fish-ing boats share the narrow inlet with expensive white yachts, and fishermen's cottages reflect in the turquoise waters. You'll also spot some caves in the cliff-side oppo-site. Even if you don't have time for all of Walk 32 today, do at least visit Cala Beltrán (**P**32).

Back at the junction (47.5km) turn right, after about 500m coming to the megalithic village of **Capocorp Vell**★ (48km ⛩; see notes and photograph opposite). After this visit to pre-history, continue along the Ma-6014 towards 'S'Estanyol' (✕ at 49km) and, at a junction (56km), go right on the Ma-6015 for a long straight run to the uninspiring resort of **S'Estanyol** (60km ✕). Keep straight on down to the seafront. Turn left, past a string of characterless houses facing the rocky sea-front, and eventually come to **Sa Ràpita** (61km ✕), where the yacht club seems to be the only sign of life.

Keeping ahead, you meet the Ma-6030, leading you away from the coast and into the country once more. At 65km turn right for 'Ses Covetes'; this narrow country lane meanders between old stone farmhouses where prickly pear cacti ramble at random. At the T-junction go right again, follow-ing a wider road back to the coast and **Ses Covetes** (68km ✕). There is a car park near the end of the road for busy days in summer, otherwise drive to the end and go right, to park somewhere near the chained off entrance to this beau-tiful white beach, stretching away into the distance. If it's hot, you'll

want to swim, or have a meal at the Ran de Mar restaurant (very good *paella*). Alternatively, go back to the road, and head right onto the other side of the headland, past half-finished beach chalets, to find the virgin beach of **Es Trenc**. This Caribbean-like beach stretches out for miles below the sand dunes, and as yet is relatively unspoilt, apart from the ugly kiosk near the beginning. Further round the bay, naturists bathe in the paradisial surroundings.
Back on asphalt and heading away from the coast once more, keep straight on past the T-junction and then veer left, following the narrow country lane as it meanders

through open countryside (rural ⛺✖ at 71km) and back round to rejoin the Ma-6030 (73km). Turn right here for a straight run into **Campos** (79km 🛉✖🚰⊕; Car tour 5). Turn left in Campos, then head straight through the town for 'Palma'. At the main road (Ma-19; 🎦), turn left for Llucmajor. This good, wide road through open countryside takes you to

Pristine Es Trenc beach (top), Capocorp Vell (middle), and flowering almond blossom. Important excavations at Capocorp Vell uncovered many valuable pieces, remains of a settlement some 3000 years ago. Although the 'finds' are now in Barcelona's Archaeological Museum and the site has unfortunately been 'tarted up' for tourists (completely destroying its natural charm), a scramble among these talayotic ruins and stone chambers affords an imaginative insight into Bronze Age communities.

Llucmajor (92km ♦✕🚌⊕M), where the 17th-century convent of Bonaventura and the 18th-century church are the main architectural highlights. By the Ma-19A, on the outskirts of the village, a stone cross indicates the site of a confrontation between the troops of Jaime III and the army of Pedro IV of Aragón. Leave Llucmajor from the first roundabout, turning right up the street where the Tiá Taleca restaurant is on the corner, and follow the signs 'Travesía' through the town (towards Algaida).

You come out on the Algaida road, the Ma-5010, once more in the countryside. At 97km turn off right up a narrow lane into **Randa** (98km ⛰♦✕), a small hillside village. Driving slowly up the narrow street, turn left just past the restaurant and then go right almost immediately, following signs 'Santuari de Cura' past the elegant Es Racó restaurant and hotel. The road winds up the **Puig de Randa** in tight bends, passing the Santuari de Gràcia (♦🏞), founded in the Middle Ages and once a travellers' hostel. Set under the brow of an enormous escarpment, it makes a beautiful setting for the open-air concerts held on some summer evenings. But it is best to visit on your way down, if it's late in the day and you want to get to the top to see the view before dusk. You pass another small oratory on the ascent — Sant

42

Honorat, on the right. Finally, at a height of 548m/ 1800ft, you arrive at the **Santuari de Cura**★ (103km ♦⛰✕🏞🔭M). Visits to the library and small chapel are a must. The ancient library contains many manuscripts, prayer books and other relics from the days of the 13th-century scholar, Ramon Llull, who was born shortly after the Reconquest of Mallorca. But apart from the historical value of the visit, there are captivating views on all sides — the southern coast with the beautiful beaches just visited, Cap Blanc, the mountains of Llevant and the monastery at Felanitx, the wide central plain, dotted with countless towns and villages, and the long chain of the Serra de Tramuntana closing off the northern horizon — all the various settings of the other car tours around the island. Alcúdia's bay is also visible on a clear day, as is the mystical isle of Cabrera to the south. Let's treat ourselves to a sundowner on the terrace, surrounded by these magnificent panoramas!

Back in Randa, leave the village via the narrow lane off right on the last bend, to rejoin the Ma-5010, and then go immediately right for 'Castellitx' along a winding country lane, through open fields and then woodlands. Come to the old church and sanctuary of **Castellitx** (112km ♦), a quiet place to stop for a leg-stretcher while you explore. Continue along the narrow lane through silent woods for quite a while, enjoying this last stretch of rural peace, until the lane opens out into **Algaida** (115km ♦✕🚌⊕). Keep straight ahead into the small square, then turn right for 'Palma'. You join the main road (Ma-15) and go left for a straight run (ample ✕🚌) back to the city (136km.).

❀ Walking

This new edition of *Landscapes of Mallorca* covers over 400km (250 miles) of some of the best walking on Mallorca. Over the years I have omitted walks which became 'spoiled' for one reason or another, in order to concentrate on the island's finest walks and making sure that the descriptions are accurate and thoroughly up-to-date. The many short walks (including the picnic suggestions) are meant to encourage beginners to take up this wonderful pastime.

I hope you'll also use this book, together with the bus, train and boat timetables on pages 131-133, to make up your own walk combinations. I've indicated where routes link up on the walking maps, and the pull-out touring map shows the general location of all the walks. One word of caution. *Never try to get from one walk to another on uncharted terrain!* Only combine walks by following paths described in these notes or by using roads or tracks: don't try to cross rough country (which might prove dangerous) or private land (where you may not have right of way).

There are walks in the book for everyone.

Beginners: Start on the walks graded 'easy' — and be sure to check all the short and alternative versions of the main walks; these are often suggestions for easier rambles. The picnic suggestions all describe superb easy walks.

Experienced walkers: If you are used to rough terrain and have a head for heights, you should be able to tackle almost all the walks in the book (a few are recommended for experts only). Naturally, you will take into account the weather conditions and their consequences. For example, if it has been raining recently, some of the mountain walks will be unsuitable. Also, *storm damage can make the way unsafe at any time.* Remember, too, always to follow the route as described in this book. If you have not reached one of the landmarks after a reasonable time, you *must* go back to the last 'sure' point and start again.

Experts: All the walks described are suitable for you — provided you always use extreme caution.

G uides, waymarking, maps

A couple of walks are graded as suitable for experts only, and I recommend that anyone other than an expert walker hire a **guide** for these routes. Not because they are particularly difficult, but because you could be suddenly overtaken by thick mists and get lost or, due to poor waymarking, you could miss the path and find yourselves in a potentially hazardous position. Guides are not easily found on the island, but you could contact: Mauricio Espinar, Carrer Almirall Cervera 23, Port de Pollença; tel: 971-864330. He speaks fluent English and French and understands some German. Otherwise you can reach me at: Carrer de Ses Monges 9, 1st floor, Santa Eugènia 07142; tel: 971-144055.

Waymarking of walks is improving. The main routes that make up the traverse of the Serra de Tramuntana are now well marked by wooden posts with white arrows and the letters 'GR' ('Gran Ruta', or long-distance walks) in red. You will come across some of these on your walks. Other than that, there is still very little signposting. Many mountain routes were marked with red paint in years past (often hard to follow today); a few routes have been waymarked with paint more recently. Another form of waymarking is the cairn — a small pile of rocks. These are placed at intervals at various points along the way; after a while you'll become accustomed to keeping a lookout for these mountain 'signs'.

The **maps** in this book have been adapted from the most recent 1:25,000 IGN and 1:50,000 military maps of the Balearics. You can buy them in advance from your usual map stockist or in Palma — at the Casa del Mapa, Carrer Santo Domingo 11 (tel/fax: 971-225945).

Right of way
Much of Mallorca is private land, and in recent years many landowners are attempting to close off routes, or parts of routes, previously open to walkers. While one can understand and sympathise with the problem of carelessly-dropped litter, open gates or uprooted crops, there does seem to be a feeling of the sierra being gradually 'closed off' — only to be enjoyed by a privileged few. Many of the routes involved are ancient pilgrims' trails, herding routes or wayfarers' roads connecting mountain villages — routes that have been freely accessible for hundreds of years.

You should not have any problems with the routes described in this book, which are all recognised rights of way. If you *do* experience any access difficulty, I would advise you to go to the 'Ajuntament' (town hall) of that particular municipality and make a complaint — or, at the very least, ask their advice. I would also ask you to walk so respectfully that landowners will not even be aware of your passing.

What to take

If you're already on Mallorca when you find this book, and you haven't any special equipment such as a rucksack, boots or a torch, you can still do some of the walks — or buy yourself some equipment at one of the sports shops on the island. Don't attempt the more difficult walks without the proper equipment! For each walk in the book, the *minimum* equipment is listed. Where walking boots are required, there is, unfortunately, no substitute: you will need to rely on the grip and ankle support they provide (many island trails are stony), as well as their waterproof qualities (in winter and spring some normally-dry streams are in flow). All other walks should be made with stout shoes, preferably with thick rubber soles, to grip on wet or slippery surfaces.

You may find the following checklist useful:

comfortable walking boots	up-to-date transport timetables
waterproof rain gear	plastic bottle, purifying tablets
long-sleeved shirt (sun protection)	long trousers, tight at the ankles
bandages, plasters, etc	suncream, sunglasses
mobile phone	knives, openers, string
windproof, two light cardigans	insect repellent
extra pair of socks and shoelaces	sunhat, plastic rainhat
small rucksack	torch, whistle, compass
plastic groundsheet	first-aid kit, safety pins, etc

Please bear in mind that I've not done *every* walk in this book under *all* weather conditions, and I may not realise just how hot — or wet — some walks might be. Your good judgement will help you to modify the equipment list according to the season.

Weather

The weather on Mallorca can be quite variable. It can be very cold in winter — but not necessarily so. In fact, some winters are pleasantly mild. It is swelteringly hot and humid from July to September. The most unreliable months are March/April and September/October, when the capricious spring and autumn rains arrive.

Most people will find it far too hot in summer for any of the strenuous walks in this book. But one of the walks, Walk 19 (the Torrent de Pareis, only negotiable after a long period without rain) is really only suitable for the summer months. Both Walk 18 (Mirador de Ses Barques to Sa Calobra) and Walk 19 rely on the Sa Calobra boat connection, which runs all year round. The service is reliable in summer, but subject to weather conditions in winter: should you want to do either of these walks outside summer, check in advance if the boats are running; call Tramuntana Boats (tel: 971-633109).

Generally the **best walking months** are January and February, perhaps March and April — if it's not too wet, May and early June, September and October — likewise, if it's not too wet, November and December. These are rough guidelines, and it sometimes seems that every year proves to be an exception! Freak weather, with heavy snow on the sierra, is not unknown in May...

A weather report with meteorological maps is given in the daily newspapers and on television every evening after the main news. You can also telephone for 'Información Meteorológica' 24 hours a day (tel: 906-365307). But be warned: the recorded message is in Spanish. Also the Meteorology Office in C/Moll de Ponent (tel: 971-403511) will inform you of any last-minute details of weather conditions.

Dogs and other nuisances

You'll encounter **dogs** at all the farms, almost always chained up. It is a good idea for each walker always to carry a stout stick, but *never* wave the stick about to menace the dogs. Moreover, always go *quietly* through all private land, leaving gates *exactly* as you find them. Only resort to your stick when confronted by an unchained and obviously unfriendly dog. (If you wish to invest in an ultrasonic dog deterrent, the Dog Dazer, contact Sunflower Books, who sell them.) There are four types of **snakes** on the island, some of them growing to about 1-1.5 metres/yards long — but none is dangerous to man. We also have **scorpions**, but these are tiny (4 centimetres/1.5 inches). They might sting you, but you won't come to any harm. More troublesome are **mosquitoes** and **ticks**. Always carry insect repellent and, when walking in dense undergrowth, it's always wise to wear long trousers, with your socks pulled up round the trouser legs, and a long-sleeved shirt.

Walkers' checklist

The following points cannot be stressed too often:

- **At any time a walk may become unsafe** due to heavy storms. If the route is not as described in this book, and your way ahead is not secure, do not attempt to go on.
- **Walks recommended for experts only** may be unsuitable in winter or after storms, or may be very wet after heavy rain. (In mild winters, all the walks are possible.)
- **Never walk alone**; four is the best walking group.
- **Do not overestimate your energies**; your speed will be determined by the slowest walker in your group.
- **Transport** connections at the end of a walk are vital.
- **Proper shoes** or boots are a necessity.

- **Mists** can suddenly appear on the higher mountains.
- **Warm clothing** is needed on the mountains; even in summer take some along, just in case you are delayed.
- **Compass, whistle, torch** weigh little, but might save your life.
- **Extra rations** must be taken on long walks.
- **Always take a sunhat** with you, and in summer a cover-up for your arms and legs as well.
- **A stout stick** is a help on rough terrain and for discouraging the rare unchained, menacing dog.
- **Do not panic** in an emergency.
- Read and re-read the *'Important note'* on page 2 and the country code on page 48, as well as guidelines on grade and equipment for each walk you plan to take.

Where to stay

Many people will be staying in or around Palma during their holiday on the island. From the capital a good public transport system permits daily travel to most parts of Mallorca. For this reason, all the walks are written up to include transport to and from Palma (however, timetables for buses from other holiday bases are also included).

Whereas the capital is your best choice if you're relying on public transport, if you plan to rent a car you have a far greater choice of locations — especially if you plan to take only short or easy walks.

If you intend to do a lot of hiking, remember that most of the island's best walks lie along the mountain chain stretching from Valldemossa to Pollença. Good centres for walks are therefore Sóller and its port and Pollença and its port. This is especially so in summer, when the bus is running at good intervals along the Ma-10 mountain road between Sóller and Pollença (see Timetable 9, page 133); many of the walks then lie within easy reach.

Briefly, if you're planning to do a lot of walking, are *pre-booking a package holiday,* and will rely on public transport, **Palma** is your best centre. **Pollença** and **Sóller** (and their ports) are also good choices.

For those *not* booking 'all-in' holidays, there is the inter-esting alternative of staying at one of Mallorca's sanctuaries, many of which offer accommodation.

Lluc, a large monastery steeped in history and set in romantic surroundings high in the mountains (photographs page 110), is placed just at the centre of some of the best island walks. Visitors may stay overnight — or for as long as they wish — in accommodation run by the friars. Buses connect Lluc with Palma direct and with Inca (from where there are hourly trains to Palma). There are also buses to Sóller and Pollença — so there's no need to feel 'cut off from civilisation'.

The next best base for such accommodation is Pollença, where the small sanctuary of **Sa Mare de Deu** atop the Puig de Maria offers modest and inexpensive accommodation in spotless rooms with breathtaking views. Many other sanctuaries take in visitors, including: the **Monastery of Cura** (above Randa); the **Sanctuary of Sant Salvador** (near Felanitx); the **Sanctuary of Monti-Sion** (near Porreres); the **Sanctuary of Bonany** (near Petra), the **Oratori de la Bona Pau** on the Puig de Sant Miquel (near Montuïri), the **Ermita de Valldemossa**, **Sant Honorat** (just below the Monastery of Cura), the **Oratori del Puig de Santa Magdalena** (near Inca) and the **Santuari de la Mare de Déu de Gràcia** (near Llucmajor). Finally, don't forget that there is good hostel accommodation atop the **Puig d'Alaró** (Walk 14) and at the mountain refuge of **Tossals Verds** (Walk 21).

A country code for walkers and motorists

The experienced rambler is used to following a 'country code', but the tourist out for a lark may unwittingly cause damage, harm animals, and even endanger his own life. A country code is especially important on Mallorca, where you often cross private land, and where the rugged terrain can lead to dangerous mistakes.

- **Only light fires** at picnic areas with fireplaces.
- **Do not frighten animals**. The goats and sheep you may encounter on your walks are not tame. By making loud noises or trying to touch or photograph them, you may cause them to run in fear and be hurt.
- **Walk quietly** through all farms and take care not to provoke the dogs. Ignore their barking and keep your walking stick out of their sight — remember, it is only to be shown to an unfriendly, unchained dog.
- **Leave all gates just as you found them**, whether they are at farms or on the mountainside. Although you may not see any animals, the gates do have a purpose — generally to keep goats or sheep in (or out of) an area.
- **Protect all wild and cultivated plants**. Don't try to pick wild flowers or uproot saplings. Obviously fruit and other crops are someone's private property and should not be touched. *Never walk over cultivated land*.
- **Take all your litter away with you.**
- *Do not take risks!* This is the most important point of all. Do not attempt walks beyond your capacity, and do not wander off the paths described if there is any sign of mist or if it is late in the day. **Never walk alone**, and *always* tell a responsible person *exactly* where you are going and when you expect to return. Remember, if you become lost or injure yourself, it may be a long time before you are found. On all long walks, carry a whistle, torch, extra water and warm clothing — as well as some high-energy food, like chocolate.

Organisation of the walks

I hope that the book is set out so that you can plan your walks easily — depending on how far you want to go, your abilities and equipment, and the season. Wherever you are based on the island, there should be a walk within relatively easy reach — and almost all the suggested walks are accessible by public transport.

You might begin by considering the large fold-out touring map inside the back cover of the book. Here you can see at a glance the overall terrain, the road network, and the location of all the walks. Quickly flipping through the book, you'll find that there's at least one photograph for every walk.

Having selected one or two potential excursions from the map and the photographs, turn to the relevant walk. At the top of the page you'll find planning information: distance/time, grade, equipment, and how to get there by public or private transport. If the grade and equipment specifications are beyond your scope, don't despair! *There's always at least one short version of each walk,* and in most cases these are far less demanding of agility and equipment.

When you are on your walk, you will find that the text begins with an introduction to the overall landscape and then quickly turns to a detailed description of the route itself. The large-scale maps (all 1:50,000) have been specially annotated and set out facing the walking notes wherever possible.

Times are given for reaching certain key checkpoints. Giving times is always tricky, because they depend on so many factors, but my times fall mostly in the range 2-4km per hour, depending on the terrain. Note that these times **include only minimal stops** — to catch your breath or take a photo. Be sure to allow extra time for other breaks — picnicking, swimming, etc.

Many of the **symbols** used on the walking maps are self-explanatory, but below is a key to the most important.

═══	motorway	●▶	spring, tank, etc	■	specified building
━━━	main road	∩	aqueduct	🗔	*talaia* (see page 55)
━━	secondary road	✝✝	church.chapel	∩¥	cave.windmill
━━	minor road	✝	shrine or cross	✕	quarry, mine
📖	map continuation	⊡	cemetery	⋀	rock formation
────	track	⊼	picnic tables	🏛	stadium
─ ─ ─ ─	cart track, path, trail	⛟	best views	△	campsite
2→	main walk	🚌	bus stop	⊓	ancient site
2→	alternative walk	🚗	car parking	P	picnic suggestion (see pages 10-15)
─ · ─ ·	watercourse, pipe	🚂	railway station	⋮	danger; danger of vertigo
400	height in metres	🏰	castle, fort		

Spanish and Mallorquín

While Spanish is still the official language of Mallorca, most of the islanders speak Mallorquín amongst themselves. The regional autonomy movement has gained much ground on the island since publication of the last edition of this book, and place names are gradually being changed from Spanish to Mallorquín. Since maps and leaflets published by our regional tourist office now refer to villages, streets, and public monuments by their Mallorquín names, I have done the same, recognising that these names will prevail in future. In the rare instance where this might result in confusion, the Mallorquín is followed by the Spanish name.

Language hints for walkers and picnickers

In the tourist centres almost everyone speaks at least a little English. But once out in the countryside, a few words of Spanish will be helpful, especially if you lose your way.

Here's an (almost) foolproof way to communicate in Spanish. First, memorise the few short key questions and their possible answers, given on the next page. Then, when you have your 'mini-speech' memorised, always ask the many questions you can concoct from it **in such a way that you get a 'sí' (yes) or 'no' answer.** *Never* ask an open-ended question like 'Where is the main road?'. You won't understand the answer — especially as it's likely to be given in Mallorquín! Instead, ask the question and then *suggest the most likely answer yourself.* For instance: 'Good day, sir. Please — where is the road to Lluc? Is it straight ahead?'. Now, unless you get a 'sí', try: 'Is It to the left?'. If you go through the list of answers to your own question, you will eventually get a 'sí' response — probably with a vigorous nod of the head — and this is just that bit more reassuring than relying solely on sign language. A good phrase book is a very valuable aid, in which you will find other 'key' phrases and answers.

Following are three of the most likely situations in which you may have to practice some Spanish. The dots (...) show where you will fill in the name of your

Dwarf fan palms (Chamaerops humilis) *grace many island walks; you'll see them in the Bóquer Valley and at Aubarca (Walks 28 and 31).*

destination. The approximate pronunciation of place names
is shown in the index, on pages 134-136.

▪ Asking the way

The key questions

English	Spanish	pronounced as
Good day, sir (madam, miss).	Buenos días, señor (señora, señorita).	Boo-**eh**-nohs **dee**-ahs, sen-**yor** (sen-**yor**-ah, sen-yor-**ee**-tah).
Please — where is	Por favor — dónde está	**Poor** fah-**vor** — **dohn**-day es-**tah**
the road to ... ?	la carretera a ... ?	la cah-reh-**teh**-rah ah ... ?
the footpath to ...	la senda de ... ?	lah **sen**-dah day ... ?
the way to... ?	el camino a ... ?	el cah-**mee**-noh ah ... ?
the bus stop?	la parada de autobus?	lah pah-**rah**-dah day ow-toh-**boos**?
Many thanks.	Muchas gracias.	**Moo**-chas **gra**-thee-as.

Secondary question, leading to a yes/no answer

English	Spanish	pronounced as
Is it here?	Está aquí?	Es-**tah** ah-**kee**?
straight ahead?	todo recto?	**toh**-doh **rec**-toh?
behind?	detrás?	day-**tras**?
to the right?	a la derecha?	ah lah day-**reh**-chah?
to the left?	a la izquierda?	ah lah eeth-kee-**er**-dah?
above?	arriba?	ah-**ree**-bah?
below?	abajo?	ah-**bah**-hoh?

▪ Making arrangements with a taxi driver

English	Spanish	pronounced as
Please —	Por favor	**Poor** fah-**vor**
take us to ...	llévanos a ...	l-**yay**-vah-nos ah ...
and return	y volver	ee vol-**vair**
for us at ...	para nosotros a ...	**pah**-rah nos-**oh**-tros ah ...

(Instead of memorising hours of the day, simply point out the time when you wish him to return on your watch, and get his agreement.)

▪ Meeting a landowner who denies you access

See notes on page 55 about right of way. If you believe that you have right of way, you might ask:

English	Spanish	pronounced as
We are going to ...	Nos vamos a ...	Nos **vah**-mohs ah ...
Please —	Por favor	**Poor** fah-**vor** —
show us	muéstranos	moo-**es**-trah-nohs
the way.	el camino.	el cah-**mee**-noh.
Many thanks.	Muchas gracias.	**Moo**-chas **gra**-thee-as.

▪ Once in a while you may meet people who do not speak
Spanish. Greet them in Mallorquín and then pronounce *very
carefully* the name of the place you are looking for (see Index
for pronunciation of landmarks in this book). The Mallorquín
for 'Good morning' is *Bon dia* (Bone **dee**-ah); 'Good afternoon' is *Bonas tardas* (**Bone**-ahs **tar**-dahs).

Island customs — past and present

Some of the customs referred to in the book may be unfamiliar to walkers exploring Mallorca for the first time. I hope the following explanations will be of interest.

Caça a coll

Thrushes were once considered a great delicacy on Mallorca, and *caça a coll* (**thrush-netting** — or, literally, 'hunting at the saddle') has been a long-standing tradition in the Balearics. Thrushes arrive in late autumn and winter from colder countries, and are especially fond of olives, but are themselves prey for larger birds, such as falcons and kestrels. Thus the thrushes fly only at dusk and in the early morning — between the tops of the tall oaks, where they take refuge at night, and the lower

A bird's-eye view of thrush-netting passages, seen from the Camí de S'Arxiduc above Deià (Walk 9)

olive orchards. They tend to glide *between* the trees and not above them, so as to protect themselves from the keen eyes of the bigger birds of prey. The islanders noticed these habits and long ago devised a method of catching the birds. They thin out linear 'passages' between the trees (see photograph above) and hold a huge net (*filat*) fixed onto two long canes across the end of a passage. The *caçador* waits silently, hidden behind a bush and, when the birds fly down towards the netting, he quickly folds it over, capturing his unfortunate victims.

Since the commercialisation of these birds is now prohibited, the popular dish of *tords amb col* (thrushes roasted in cabbage leaves) can no longer be found on Mallorcan menus. Thrush-netting is still practised (it is permissible on certain days), but it seems to be on the decline because fewer and fewer thrushes migrate this way — perhaps due to changes in the climate.

Cases de neu (Spanish: casas de nieve)

The *cases de neu* ('snow houses') are deep pits, only found on the highest part of the sierra. Here snow was stored to make ice before the advent of the refrigerator.

There are many of these *cases de neu* on the mountains of Massanella, Major, Teix and Tomir.

During the winter months, when heavy snow fell on the mountains, a group of men would set out for the peaks and fill these deep, stone-walled holes with snow, packing it down hard. Once full, the pit was covered over with ashes or salt, and it remained

These ruins on the northern slopes of Massanella (Walk 22) were inhabited by the 'snowmen' who tended the nearby cases de neu.

frozen solid until the arrival of warmer weather. One man would stay behind, to tend the salt or ash covering, making repairs if necessary.

In summer, and at night, blocks of ice weighing about fifty kilos (100 lbs) were loaded onto mules and taken down into the towns and villages, where they were used not only to make ice-creams and the like, but also for medicinal purposes. The so-called *oli de neu* ('snow-oil'), which was a mixture of ice and olive oil, was used to heal wounds and was reputed to stop bleeding.

Forns de calç (Spanish: hornos de cal)

You'll see the remains of many of these **ovens** *(forns)* around Mallorca. They were used to produce **lime** *(calç)* for whitening the interiors of houses, or to be mixed with fine gravel for use in building.

The work was usually carried out by three men, labouring day and night for anything between nine and fifteen days. A great amount of heat was necessary to produce the reaction, and in these ovens an enormous quantity of wood was burned to obtain the heat required. Normally the thinner logs — which were not suitable for the charcoal industry (see *'Sitjas'* on page 55) — were used, and any amount up to two tonnes could be burnt during one 'cooking'! A normal-sized oven would produce between a hundred and a hundred and fifty tonnes of burnt lime in one session.

Santuaris (Spanish: monasterios, santuarios), Ermitas

There are many **sanctuaries** on the island. Some of them are even today the homes of hermits who lead a simple and solitary life. They remind us of medieval times, dressed in full-length brown wool habits, with their heads shaven and their long white beards.

Although much early evidence of hermit life has been discovered on Mallorca, Ramon Llull is accepted by the islanders as being the founder of the monastic life. Born a few years after the invasion of Mallorca by Jaime I in 1229, Llull was the son of a Catalan who accompanied the king during the Reconquest. Ramon Llull himself then became the steward of the future king, Jaime II, while still in his teens. Later, he married Blanca de Picany, by whom he had two children. As he grew older, however, he found that his Latin passions could not be satisfied solely by his wife, and he turned to

Below: forn de calç *near Lluc*

You can explore the vertiginous Canaleta de Massanella as an optional detour during Walk 22 (see page 109).

eaten at 12.30, the afternoon and evening are spent in prayer, self-examination, meditation and further labour. Lights are out at 21.00, and each hermit retires to his cell where he rests until, at 01.00, the day repeats itself.

The governing superior resides at the Santuari of Sant Salvador near Felanitx (Car tour 5) and is elected every six years by the hermits themselves. Novices begin their trial periods at S'Ermita de Betlem near Artà (Car tour 4).

Of special interest to lovers of the countryside (and walkers in particular) is the opportunity to stay overnight at various monasteries scattered around the island. The simple accommodation is spotless and, owing to their remote position on hilltops, the views are always superb. See also page 47, 'Where to stay'.

other lovers in search of further pleasure and deeper fulfilment. At about the age of thirty, he suddenly repented of his sins and turned to strict penitence — making pilgrimages to the sanctuaries of Santiago de Compostela and Montserrat. Back on Mallorca, in 1275 he went to Randa, living in a small grotto on the hillside. Later he founded a missionary school in Valldemossa, where oriental languages were taught to friars who would eventually travel in Asia and Africa to convert the followers of Islam. Llull was martyred in North Africa in 1315, stoned to death by Saracens. His remains were brought back to Mallorca by Genovese merchants, and his relics were placed in the Basilica of Sant Françesc in Palma.

A typical day in the life of a hermit starts at 01.00, when he rises for the first prayers of the day. A second call to prayer comes at 06.00, followed by breakfast and manual labour assigned by the superior. After the main meal is

Síquies (Spanish: canales or acequias)

These 'little canals' ('canaletas'; the Spanish name is more generally used) may still be seen around the island (see photographs above and page 57). Made of stone, they carry water from springs down the hillsides to irrigate crops. Today, most of these delightful free-flowing watercourses have been replaced by metal conduits, for sanitation reasons and to prevent evaporation — a great loss for lovers of the landscape.

The island's most famous watercourse, the *Canaleta de Massanella* (shown above), is 7km long and runs from the Font d'es Prat to Mancor del Valle. Its history is interesting. The work is attributed to a certain Montserrat Fontanet, a Mallorcan pig farmer employed on the Massanella farmholding during the 18th century. The owner of this large property had brought engineers from France, England, Italy and

Torre Picada above Sóller

the Spanish mainland, to plan and execute the channelling of waters from the Es Prat spring. All these eminent engineers agreed that such a feat was technically impossible, after which Señor Fontanet offered to do the job himself. His employer agreed to the suggestion, and the work was reportedly completed in two years — a record feat by any standards.

Sitjas (Spanish: círculo de carboneros)

Circular earthen mounds, ringed with stones and now covered in moss — *sitjas* — are the only remains of the old charcoal industry. In summer months the charcoal-makers lived with their families in the oak woods on the mountainsides. The sturdiest logs from the holm oak were used, and the fires burned round the clock, producing about one and a half tonnes of charcoal in a week. But the work was poorly paid. Sometimes the remains of a stone hut dwelling are to be found near the sitjas (see photograph on page 56).

Talaias (Spanish: atalayas)

Talaias are **ancient watchtowers**, built in the latter half of the 16th century, to guard against the frequent attacks of pirates and the ever-growing menace of invasion by the Turks.

More than thirty of these *talaias* were in action in the year 1595, and much of the credit for their strategic siting is due to the magnificent work of Juán Binimelis — an astrologer, mathematician, doctor, priest and chronicler. His vast knowledge of Mallorca's terrain, of topography, of artillery and of engineering made it possible to raise these stone outposts at the most suitable points. At the same time, other means of defence — such as Sa Torre in the Port of Alcúdia — were in the planning stages. From these high points of vigilance (sometimes also called *talaias de foc* or 'fire towers'), approaching sea-craft could be seen at a great distance, and fire and smoke signals were relayed across the island, warning of the danger. Once the enemy was sighted, the coastal inhabitants could take refuge (see notes about the Torre de Canyamel on the next page), while the alerted naval forces would immediately move to the threatened areas.

You will encounter these watch-towers all round the island, and you'll visit several of them if you take any of our island walks. But even if you only see Mallorca from a car or coach, you'll surely visit the Talaia de Ses Animes (photograph page 70), just south of Banyalbufar, now a superbly-renovated *mirador*.

Let's consider just one interesting example of this network of watchtowers in action: a relay of signals between the Talaia de Albercutx on the Formentor Peninsula (Car tour 3), the Talaia de Alcúdia and the *talaia* at Penya Rotja on the Cape of Pines (Walk 29), and the Talaia de Morey and the Torre de Aubarca in the Artà mountains (Walk 31; photographs page 128), more than adequately covered the only northern routes of entry to the island — the bays of Pollença and Alcúdia.

Top: a sitja *encountered on Walk 9.
Above, left: farm with a well (*pou*) and
a furnace for firing tiles in the background; right: the Torre de Canyamel
(Car tour 4) was built in the 14th
century over Arab and Roman
foundations; here people took refuge
during pirate sieges, once alerted by
flares from a* talaia.
*Left: a spring (*font*) and water tank
(*safareig*) at the Finca de L'Ofre
(Walk 16) is home to a duck.*

*Opposite: the old houses of Es Cosconar
(top), built into caves in the valley
below Lluc Monastery.
Middle: Arab water deposits near
Alaró Castle (Walk 14).
Right: at Ternelles, near Pollença — a
watercourse (*síquia or canaleta*) and a
balcony made from an old wine press.*

1 SANT ELM • (CALA EMBASSET) • SA TRAPA • PUNTA D'ES FABIOLET • SES BASSES • ANDRATX

See also photograph on page 63
Distance/time: 12km/7.4mi; 5h (14km/8.7mi; 5h30min if you descend to Cala Embasset)
Grade: part of the initial ascent to Sa Trapa is fairly strenuous; the rest of the walk is easy but quite long; ascents/descents totalling about 450m/1475ft and some scrambling over rocks. From Ses Basses wide tracks all the way down to Andratx.
Equipment: hiking boots, water, picnic, sunhat, binoculars; windproof/extra jumpers in winter; swimwear/suncream in summer
How to get there: 🚌 to Sant Elm (Timetable 7). If travelling by 🚗, park in Andratx and take a taxi or bus to Sant Elm to start.
To return: 🚌 from Andratx (Timetable 5)
Shorter walk: Sant Elm — Sa Trapa — Sant Elm. 7km/4.3mi; 2h45min; grade and equipment as above (ascents of about 350m/1150ft). 🚌 or 🚗 to/from Sant Elm. Follow the main walk to Sa Trapa (1h05min). To return, keep uphill on the wide track from Sa Trapa, over the mountain pass, then descend to a fork (2h10min), where you turn right for Sant Elm (signposted).

About 7km along the winding country road from Andratx, on the westernmost point of the island, lies Sant Elm. A quiet seaside village in winter, a busy little resort in summer, it looks out towards the rocky island of Sa Dragonera across a narrow stretch of deep blue water. There are many lovely woodland walks in this area, but most interesting is the ascent to the ruins of an ancient Trappist monastery set among almond tree terraces high up on the cliff-tops. The route then continues along rugged red cliffs with magnificent coastal views (one can see as far as Sóller or even further on a clear day), before turning inland across some of the quietest, least inhabited hills on the island. Finally we descend a green and fertile valley into the town of Andratx.

From the BUS STOP in the Plaça Mossén Sebastià Grau (the last stop) in **Sant Elm**, **begin the walk** by going up left to the Avinguda Sa Trapa, signposted 'SA TRAPA, CA'N TOMEVÍ, CALA EMBASSET'. Follow this road towards the woods. The tarmac soon ends, and the way becomes an earthen track. In **15min** you'll reach a house, **Ca'n Tomeví**. Here the track divides: to the left is the short route described on page 11, up to the watchtower above Cala Embasset (**Torre de Cala Embasset**; Picnic 1; photographs page 10 and overleaf), while to the right lies the longer way up to Sa Trapa (Walk 2). On this walk we follow the 'CALA EMBASSET' signposting straight ahead (to the left of the big sign and map on the tree), in two minutes rising to a wider path where two stone posts indicate the way down to Cala Embasset.* Continue ahead up a

*If you are agile and not too burdened with heavy rucksacks, you might like to turn left here (between two stone posts) and make your way down to **Cala Embasset** for a swim. It takes about 15 minutes to reach this delightful sheltered little rocky cove, *but note that* the bottom 7m/20ft of the path has fallen away. On your return from the beach, turn left just beyond the posts, and rejoin the main walk up to Sa Trapa.

58

well-defined, cairn-marked path, which soon becomes steeper, coming out of the trees higher up with good views down over the bay of Sant Elm and across to the isle of Dragonera. The path levels out for a short while further up (**35min**), climbs the side of another cliff, levels out again, and finally climbs the last rocky slope. Near the top of this last ridge, look carefully for the paint spots indicating a sharp turn right up between some high boulders (if you miss this you´ll come to a rather precipitous edge!), and scramble up a 'path' amongst the rocks, eventually reaching the top by a large sign (unfortunately only in Mallorcan) welcoming you to the area. The path now descends gently to **Sa Trapa** (**1h05min**).

The old monastery buildings are set back from the cliff-edge on a series of sloping grassy terraces planted with almond trees. Trappist monks lived here until the end of the 18th century, when the Spanish government abolished many of these institutions for both political and financial reasons. Now it is owned by the Balearic Ornithological Group (GOB), who are restoring the main building for use as a refuge for hikers. (One can spend the night here; tel: 971-721105 for information.) Walk past the monastery and round past the old millhouse opposite (also restored), and continue to the cliff-edge. Do be careful of the unprotected drop: a young Mallorcan met an untimely death here; you can see the memorial stone placed at the viewpoint by the family. Back at the monastery, you will find plenty of good spots to take elevenses or have an early picnic lunch under the almond trees.

The route continues up the wide track behind the monastery. Some 7-8 minutes up, on a wide bend, take the obvious narrow path off left (a wooden sign to S'ARRACÓ points in the opposite direction). This undulates along the hillside, gradually rising. At a faint fork, with an arrow at ground level (**1h40min**), keep left, contouring towards the sea along a winding rocky path. Coming to a really large CAIRN AT A JUNCTION (**1h50min**), keep left, towards the sea. In a few minutes you reach the amazing walled-in lookout atop the **Punta d'es Fabiolet**, shown on page 63. From here you enjoy a fantastic 'aerial' views of the isle of Sa Dragonera. *Take extra care* at this vertiginous spot, please! Although the viewpoint is walled-in, the wall is low, and

Cala Embasset

there is a sheer drop to the sea some 400m/1300ft below. Return to the cairn and keep left, to continue along the stony path. Watch your footing on this path but, five minutes further along, pause a moment to enjoy a marvellous view along a great stretch of the northwestern coast-line — it really is a beautiful sight. You can also see the rounded summit of S'Esclop (Walk 6, photograph pages 72-73) dominating the horizon high above the coast.

Now the path begins to descend gradually, and it eventually turns inland. Keep right at the first little clump of trees, and follow the path which soon widens out. Not long after passing an old house up on the left, you come to an abandoned house with a front

porch at **Ses Basses (2h15min)**. This is also a pleasant, quiet place to picnic, sitting on the old stone seat in the porch, with the lonely hills and valleys unfolding away into the distance. The southwest coastline, with the islets of El Toro near Peguera and Santa Ponça, is also visible from here.

After either a picnic or a drink stop, continue down the wide track past the house. The track bends to the right and left. *(On the first straight stretch, the track off to the right, by the cairn, is the return route to S'Arracó for Walk 2.)* The track then continues for about another 45 minutes over the solitary hills (keep left at **2h40min**, where the track has descended to the woods). The way then becomes an earthen track, and a pleasantly easy walk through

60

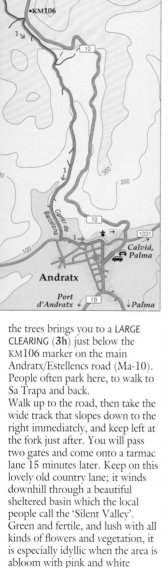

the trees brings you to a LARGE CLEARING (**3h**) just below the KM106 marker on the main Andratx/Estellencs road (Ma-10). People often park here, to walk to Sa Trapa and back.

Walk up to the road, then take the wide track that slopes down to the right immediately, and keep left at the fork just after. You will pass two gates and come onto a tarmac lane 15 minutes later. Keep on this lovely old country lane; it winds downhill through a beautiful sheltered basin which the local people call the 'Silent Valley'. Green and fertile, and lush with all kinds of flowers and vegetation, it is especially idyllic when the area is abloom with pink and white almond blossom in January or early February!

You come into **Andratx** along the

Negotiating the rocks near the top of the last ridge, before descending to Sa Trapa; the island of Sa Dragonera is in the background (top). Among the many wild flowers gracing the path you'll find the tiny scarlet pimpernel (Anagallis arvensis).

Carrer de Barcelona at **4h20min**. At the end, turn left along the main road (Ma-1030). Go right and follow the main road to the end, turning down again to find the beginning of the Ma-10 (sign-posted to Estellencs) off left. Turn left up this road, to find the BUS STOP and car park on the right (**5h**).

61

2 S'ARRACO • SA TRAPA • PUNTA D'ES FABIOLET • SES BASSES • S'ARRACO

See map pages 60-61
Distance/time: 13km/8mi; 5h
Grade: part of the ascent to Sa Trapa is fairly strenuous; the rest of the walk is easy but quite long; ascents/descents totalling about 350m/1150ft. From Ses Basses wide tracks or good paths back to S'Arracó.
Equipment: hiking boots, water, picnic, sunhat, binoculars; windproof and extra jumpers in winter; swimwear and suncream in summer

How to get there and return:
🚌 to/from S'Arracó (Timetable 7 or *summer only* service running between Sant Elm and S'Arracó every two hours; enquire in advance at a tourist office), or 🚗 to/from S'Arracó (park by the school in the Camí d'es Castellas, where the walk ends).

Short walk: S'Arracó — Puig Basset — S'Arracó. 4.5km/2.8mi; 2h; ascent — initially easy, but the last half hour is steep. Access/return as the main walk (by car, park at the cemetery by the KM5 marker on the Ma-1030). Equipment: stout walking shoes, water, picnic or snack; windproof in winter. **Start out** by following the main walk as far as the CEMETERY, where you turn right on the lane at the back of the parking area. Cut off right

onto a dirt track almost immediately, descending past a little house with solar panels. Keep ahead (left) down a narrow earthen path, and then ascend gently to pass a STONE HUT (**10min**). Just beyond the hut, follow the path down left, and at an obvious point descend left again to pass a SMALLER, RUINED HUT (**15min**). Now the narrow path winds through overgrown fields; shortly you cross a STREAM-BED and rise up onto a wider path. This descends left (**25min**; cairn-marked) and crosses the streambed again. Once on the far bank, follow the narrow path — rising gently at first, but later more steeply. Notice the interesting rock formations up ahead. You round the HEAD OF A GULLY and climb steeply to a grassy slope (**35min**). Go up left, following the cairns, and making for the shelter visible up to the left. Once at the STONE SHELTER (**1h**), a couple more minutes up the steps to the left will bring you to the fabulous viewpoint perched on the edge of **Puig Basset** (Picnic 2), with splendid panoramic views over Sant Elm, its bay, the surrounding mountains and valleys, and the jagged rocky Isle of Dragonera. Return the same way to the CEMETERY (**2h**).

This walk approaches Sa Trapa from the enchanting village of S'Arracó, nestling in a sheltered valley at the far south-western end of the Serra de Tramuntana. The fairly long but pleasant circuit combines fine coastal views with silent, lonely foothills, before we return through lower woodlands to S'Arracó.

Begin the walk at **S'Arracó**: walk towards SANT ELM on the Ma-1030. Walk past the CEMETERY on the right (at KM5) and continue round the next double bend, to come to the CAMÍ SA FONT DELS MORERS on the right (**20min**), signposted to

SA TRAPA. Take this wide stony track, ignoring a steep turn up right a minute later. On the first bend you have excellent views left over the bay of Sant Elm and can also see the old watchtower atop the jagged peak crowning the Isle

Descending to Sa Trapa

of Dragonera. Ignore a track off left (**30min**); veer right along main route, which soon begins to ascend gently. You pass a pleasant picnic spot off right under some pines (**50min**) just before coming to a junction where a left leads to San Telm along the Camí Punta Sa Galera. Keep right towards SA TRAPA (signposted) along the CAMÍ COLL DELS CAIRATS. Keep ahead at the next junction (small wooden sign on a tree left off the track). You eventually wind up steeply over the coll and descend to **Sa Trapa** (**1h55min**).

Now follow Walk 1 from the 1h05min-point, via the VIEWPOINT above the **Punta d'es Fabiolet**, to the house at **Ses Basses** (**2h 45min**). Wind down and, some five minutes below the house, turn sharp right on a descending track (cairn), zigzagging down into a valley. The wide track ends at the bottom just before a DAM (**3h05min**). Veer slightly right here, to climb an easily-seen walled-in path up the slopes of the **Puig de Corso**. This is a magnificent part of the walk — silent hills and valleys all around and not a sign of civilisation!

As you come over the top, rounding the head of a valley, there's a panoramic view across to where you were walking earlier. The cairned route descends past a small STONE HUT IN RUINS (**3h45min**). Well below the hut the path turns right and becomes rockier (ignore faint offshoots), still descending. It passes between the ruins of an old stone wall and enters the woods (**4h**). As you rise towards a coll, there is a lovely place to rest off to the right — an open grassy area edged by an unusual rock wall, pretty with tall pink asphodels in spring.

Crossing the coll (**4h20min**) the path becomes a wide stony track. Ten minutes down, turn sharp right (**4h30min**) and *again* sharp right (cairned), descending past a couple of houses. Some 10 minutes later, on a very wide bend to the left, take the obvious path straight ahead through the trees (RED MARK, CAIRN). Go through a rickety wooden gate and continue along the narrow path between fences. Turn left on a wider track at the end, and keep on the main route, winding down to a metalled road. Turn right to walk down into **S'Arracó**, coming onto the CAMÍ D'ES CASTELLAS. Continue down to the main road and turn up left to the BUS STOP (**5h**).

3 GALATZO ASCENT FROM SA FONT D'ES PI

Distance/time: 7km/4.3mi; 3h
Grade: moderate ascent of 400m/1300ft, requiring stamina (there is a very rocky scree to cross, and some scrambling up high rocks near the summit).
Equipment: hiking boots or strong shoes, water, picnic, sunhat; windproof and warm clothing in winter
How to get there and return: 🚌 to/from the Font d'es Pí above Puigpunyent. Coming into Puigpunyent from Palma, turn left on the road to Galilea. After about 200m turn right on a tarmac lane

signposted to 'La Reserva' (note your km reading here). Keep following 'La Reserva' signs uphill until you reach a wide three-way fork, where the entrance to 'La Reserva' descends the middle option: keep right here. Veer left some 900m above the fork (red arrow on a rock on a bend), later passing a small quarry and a rough track rising steeply to the right (this also leads to the *font,* but is not fit for cars). 4.9km from the first signpost, turn up sharp right for some 400m, to park in the clearing by the Font d'es Pí.

The hike up the rocky Galatzó mountain, shown on page 69, can be surprisingly easy — or a real challenge. Whichever route you choose (Walks 3-5), your reward will be a spectacular panorama down over the western coastline and Palma and, to the northeast, across the mountain peaks that comprise the Serra de Tramuntana, with the fertile plain stretching away below to the south. This ascent from the Font d'es Pí is decidedly easier than it appears when you look up at the rugged mountain from below. It is considerably less demanding than the ascent of Tomir, and children who are used to hiking will love this mountain adventure!

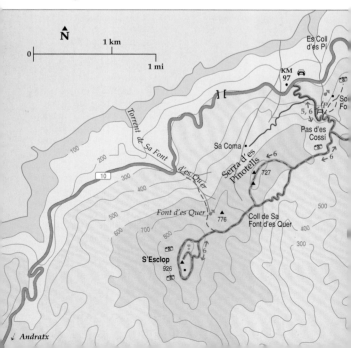

Start out at Sa Font d'es Pí: climb the wide track edged by a wire-mesh fence. At a fork (**3min**), take the stony track on the right. Two minutes later, fork left on a narrow path. This well-waymarked woodland path winds gently uphill and then rises more sharply, eventually coming out of the trees onto the bare, fire-ravaged slopes below the **Coll d'es Carniceret**. About **30min** up you will reach the brow of the hill (Picnic 3), and what a wonderful surprise will greet you when you glimpse the view over the other side, down over the green slopes of Estellencs, a pretty village caught between the mountains and the coast! Hopefully it is clear — floating mists can often hang around this north side of Galatzó. From this point, you will also be able to see the second stage of the walk — the narrow continuing path to the left: it descends to cross a scree and then rises again, rounding the north face of the mountain and climbing to a second ridge. Follow this, taking care across the scree, where some of the rocks are wobbly. The ridge of **Es Pas de Na Sabatera** (1h) is a good place to take a break before tackling the third, most strenuous stage of the hike. (The path coming up the other side of the ridge is the ascent route for both Walks 4 and 5).

The final stretch begins from behind the ruins of the old STONE REFUGE here on the ridge. Follow the rocky path, which is fairly steep in places; the way is sporadically marked with red paint, and some cairns. After clambering up some high rocks near the top, veer left and come to the SUMMIT OF **Galatzó** (1h40min). Unless you are unlucky enough to be caught literally with your head in the clouds, I would say that this is one of the best vantage points from which to contemplate the sierra — a rugged horizon of rocky peaks stretching away into the distance. Descend the same way; it takes about 1h20min to come back down to the clearing and your car at the **Font d'es Pí** (3h).

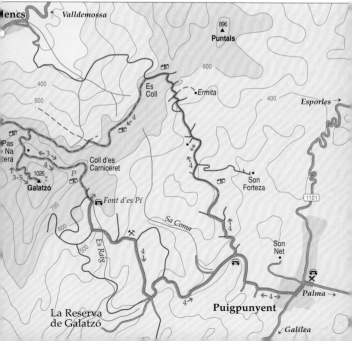

See map pages **64-65**
Distance/time: 14km/8.7mi; 6-7h
Grade: not technically difficult,
but a strenuous climb of about
750m/2460ft — and long; you
need to be really fit to do this hike.
Note also that just over 5km is on
(quiet) tarmac lanes.
Equipment: hiking boots or
strong shoes, water, picnic,

sunhat; windproof and warm
clothing in winter, extra food and
water.
How to get there and return: 🚌
to Puigpunyent. Either park at the
Son Net restaurant (at the
entrance to Puigpunyent when
coming from Palma) or park at the
25min-point in the walk (reducing
the walking time by about 1h).

While Walk 3 is the most popular approach to summit of
Galatzó, this hike is a strenuous challenge which should
only be tackled by the very fit. You'll have a rocky ascent up
to the col of Na Sabatera, a brief respite of level walking round
the ridges (with stunning coastal views), then another rocky
ascent to the summit — a five-star hike in every sense.

Start out from the SON NET
RESTAURANT CAR PARK (or continue by car). Walk up to the STOP
sign and turn left on the road
signposted to GALILEA. After about
200m/yds turn right (signposted
'La Reserva'). Now follow 'La
Reserva' signs for about 1.4km
(just under a mile), when you will
come to a widening in the road,
where there are some rubbish
containers on the left (**25min**;
motorists can park here, well
tucked in).
Here take a sharp right U-turn
down the lane; at the next fork,
head up to the left. This wide
tarmac lane winds up the hillside
between chalets and little houses
(keep right at a first fork, left a few
minutes later, and then right
again). On this last bend, a
cacophony of barking dogs will
accompany you to the top! The
TARMAC ENDS (**55min**), and you
continue up some rough steps cut
into the earth, to the right.
Keeping alongside the wire fence,
you come to a stone wall with
built-in steps and a WOODEN
LADDER-STILE. On the other side,
veer slightly left along the narrow
path, which soon levels out and
widens. Here there is a good view
down right through the trees over

a beautiful example of a 16th-
century Mallorcan aristocratic
mansion, **Son Forteza**. Elevated
on terraces above Puigpunyent
and surrounded by orange and
lemon groves, its romantic
landscaped gardens boast an impressive waterfall approached by a
pergola with 76 columns and a
natural lake (not visible from
here). Don Felipe Villalonga i
Fuster de Puigdorfila, a direct
descendent of a Spanish noble, still
lives there. At the fork, keep down
to the right, and at **1h10min** join
the MAIN ROUTE THAT COMES UP
FROM SON FORTEZA.
Now turn up left and continue
along the main track, through this
very peaceful and picturesque
landscape of open terraces, passing
a freshwater SPRING. At **1h25min**,
just after a sharp bend to the left,
take the track up to the right (the
continuing track leads to an
abandoned house). Go right again
just before a gap in the stone wall;
from here onwards there are some
CAIRNS AND RED PAINT WAY-
MARKING. Soon go through a
gateway. At the next fork
(**1h30min**) keep up to the left and
then continue straight ahead, at
1h37min going through a gate
(please close it behind you). Now

Winter: Puigpunyent from the road to Sa Font d'es Pí

turn right; you will see a red arrow on the wall opposite. Walk alongside a stone wall, soon coming up to a wide track. Cross it and follow the red paint marks up through the woods. When you come up to another wide track, follow it uphill to the right. You will pass by a gap in the stone wall (**1h50min**); it is the entrance to an old *ermita,* and you can see the abandoned building sitting on the terraces if you look over the wall a little further uphill. On the first Sunday after Easter, all the villagers from Puigpunyent come up to this *ermita* for a picnic, on the so-called 'Day of the Angels'. Keep up left at the next fork, and then continue straight ahead, always following the red paint spots and cairns.

At **2h10min** turn up sharp left (red spot on a tree trunk); another few minutes will bring you up to a level stretch, where the route, now less rocky, becomes a pleasant earthen track through the silent oak woods. You may like to look at one or two old stone wood-cutters' dwellings hiding in the trees along here, to the left and right. Climb the WOODEN LADDER-STILE over the dividing wall of **Es**

Coll (**2h20min**), and immediately, if it is clear, you will see the little village of Estellencs nestling at the foot of the mountains far below you, and enjoy a superb outlook over a stretch of the rugged northwestern coastline. Time for a photo or three!

Continue on down the easy, wide track to the left for about 200m/yds; then, on a bend, *look carefully* for the faint earthen path going off left through the trees (some cairns here). This is your route, and you will now follow this narrow path through the trees for about half an hour, rounding the contours of these high wooded slopes, with excellent coastal views and some stunning views of our friend the Galatzó mountain — from this viewpoint it looks quite impressive — like a smaller version of the Matterhorn! Some 20 minutes along, a sheltered rocky clearing to the right of the path makes a good picnic spot, with large stone slabs useful as a 'table' — but note that there is also an excellent picnic area in a clearing 15 minutes further up. At **2h55min** go through a gap in an old stone wall, after which the

path descends a little gully.
A couple of minutes later, just where the path begins to ascend again, look very carefully for the beginning of your somewhat arduous ascent to the peak — it's a camouflaged little earthen path that goes up to the left (some small cairns here). Climbing through rough scrubs, this fairly overgrown path becomes steeper and stonier, and rises for about 10 minutes (keep to the right of the trees bordering the crest, with Galatzó straight ahead of you). You will come up to a level stretch, where there is a CLEARING (**3h10min**); this is my favourite picnic place on the hike. It's very

tempting to take a *siesta* after eating, but there's quite a steep climb ahead, so better continue! To leave the clearing, veer right, behind the bushes, and follow the path which winds through the trees and goes through a gap in another stone wall, after which it crosses a *sitja*.
Now you start to climb in earnest, and eventually come up to a SIGNPOSTED MOUNTAIN CROSS-ROADS at **3h45min**. Here another path comes in through a rocky pass to the right (this is the ascent route of Walk 5 and also leads to the magnificent S'Esclop mountain which is visited on Walk 6). The onward route to the Galatzó peak

Galatzó from the Valldemossa–Puigpunyent road

Galatzó from the south

makes a U-turn up to the left here, rising above the incoming trail. As you climb higher, take a breather to admire the absolutely spectacular scenery all around; it is truly breathtaking! Twenty minutes more will bring you to a second mountain pass, the **Pas de Na Sabatera** (**4h05min**); there is room to sit for a minute on the ruins of what used to be a mountain hut and recuperate energy for the final assault.

At this point you join Walk 3 at the 1h-point; pick up the notes on page 65. On this approach you reach the SUMMIT OF **Galatzó** in **4h45min**.

To return to Puigpunyent, come back down to the Pas de Na Sabatera and turn right, following the narrow descending path and crossing the scree *with care*. You will rise to the next ridge, the **Coll d'es Carniceret**, at **5h25min**. Then take the path down the opposite side, towards the bare hill with a stone wall across it. You will eventually come down to the

woods and, further down, onto the wide stony lane which leads to the **Font d'es Pí** spring (where Walk 3 begins and ends; **5h45min**). From here, keep left and, on coming down to the tarmac road ten minutes later, go left again. Now you have a 5km-long walk along a (quiet) tarmac lane, and you will soon pass a small quarry. At the next junction go straight ahead. At the following junction, keep left again, passing the entrance to La Reserva on your right. Winding downhill, you will arrive back at your parked car at **6h15min** — or at **6h35min**, if you parked at the SON NET RESTAURANT.

5 GALATZO ASCENT FROM NEAR ESTELLENCS

See map pages 64-65 and
photographs pages 68, 69
Distance/time: 10km/6.2mi; 5h
Grade: strenuous; a steep ascent
of about 800m/2625ft overall
Equipment: hiking boots, plenty
of water, picnic, sunhat, suncream,
whistle; extra clothing, windproof
and woollen hat in winter.
How to get there and return: 🚌
to KM97 on the Ma-10 at
Estellencs; park well off the road.
(Note: If you have a 4WD vehicle,
there are several good parking
areas up the steep track where the
walk begins).

Although not the longest of my three routes up Galatzó,
this walk is every bit as strenuous as Walk 4. But it offers
unsurpassed views all the way up, and brings about a well-
deserved feeling of achievement at the end of the day — so if
you're bursting with vitality, why not take up the challenge?

Begin at KM97 on the *Ma-10*; a
large sign ('SON FORTUNY')
minute up the wide track indicates
the beginning of the route. Follow
the notes for Walk 6 opposite as
far as the **Pas d'es Cossi** (**45min**).
Then turn left to continue on a less
demanding path that ascends
much more gently, just below the
flat-topped rocky hill known as the
'**Moleta Rasa**' (the 'flat-topped
elevation'). Cross a torrent
depression by a stone well and,
soon after, a very impressive view
of the huge rocky massif of
S'Esclop (photograph pages 72-
73) fills the southwestern horizon.
Once over the ridge, S'Esclop
disappears, and you are confronted
with her neighbour, the enormous
jagged triangular peak of Galatzó.
The trail now crosses a small
prairie dotted with spiky pampas
grass, rosemary scrubs and some
sporadic clumps of pine woods.
There are far-reaching views to the
sloping pine-covered Puntals
mountain (896m/2940ft)
towering above Estellencs to the
left. Further on, a shady clump of
trees by some large rocks makes a

pleasant picnic spot. Continue
along the trail; it descends slightly
before starting to rise again
through the trees, and soon
becomes a narrow rocky path.
At **1h35min** it comes up onto the
tail-end of a level stretch of stony
path, by a small solitary pine. Turn
left, rising a few minutes later to a
SIGNPOSTED MOUNTAIN CROSS-
ROADS (**1h40min**), where you
join Walk 4. Pick up those notes at
the 3h45min-point (page 69), to
reach the SUMMIT OF **Galatzó**
(**2h40min**) where, somewhat
breathless, but loving every minute,
your efforts will be repaid in full!
Descend via the same route to
KM97 on the *Ma-10* (**5h**).

*The dramatically-sited Talaia de Ses
Animes is just north of Estellencs. It has
been refurbished since this photograph
was taken and is now a superb mirador
overlooking the coast and the terraces at
Banyalbufar (Car tour 1).*

6 S'ESCLOP

See map pages 64-65
Distance/time: 12km/7.4mi; 6-7h
Grade: moderate, with a climb
and descent of about 650m/
2130ft. Only recommended for
the intrepid trail-finder, however:
the path is somewhat difficult to
distinguish at times, although
there are cairns. The summit is
rough and surrounded by a rocky
wilderness, and should not be
climbed by the inexperienced. Not
recommended in changeable
weather conditions.
Equipment: hiking boots, water,
picnic, compass, whistle, suncream
and sunhat, extra rations;
windproof and warm clothing in
winter
How to get there and return: 🚌
to KM97 on the Ma-10 at
Estellencs. Park by the main road,
well tucked in. (Note: Those with
4WD vehicles can park up the
beginning of the steep track
followed in the walk.)

The 'lost world' of S'Esclop is a wonderful adventure!
However, it is not for the inexperienced; the extensive
stretch between the Galatzó and S'Esclop mountains is a
wilderness of rocks, rough scrubs and high pampas grass, an
impressive but lonely landscape, with but a few goat trails,
and hardly any shelter in a storm. Yet the panoramic views
from the summit surpass all expectations! So, if you're a hardy
hiker and love adventure, join me in this challenge — I
guarantee a superb day's walking!

Start the walk on the steep wide
track that begins at KM97 on the
Andratx/Estellencs road (Ma-10).
At large sign ('SON FORTUNY'), a
minute up, indicates the beginning
of the route. At **15min** turn left at
a fork, as indicated by a WOODEN
SIGN. The track levels out, then
dips and rises through the woods,
and winds up left to the **Son
Fortuny** PICNIC SITE (**25min**;
Picnic 6). Ignore the track ahead
through the gateway here (signposted to Ses Serveres); go right,
to walk up through the picnic area.
You will pass a typical wood-
cutters' dwelling complete with
thatched roof, and come to a wide
trail signposted 'GALATZO — PAS
D'ES COSSI'. Follow this trail sharp
right uphill. It soon becomes a
narrow rocky path, winding up
steeply between two reddish
escarpments.
At **45min** you come up to the **Pas
d'es Cossí**, and another wooden
signpost: 'Galatzó' is to the left
(the route of Walk 5); 'S'ESCLOP',

today's destination, is to the right.
You now climb a narrow trail
marked with some YELLOW PAINT
SPOTS — essential for route finding
here, as various little paths head
uphill. Come up to a ROCKY CAIRN
at **55min**; it marks the top of the
ridge. Opposite the cairn, 'PAS
D'ES COSSI' and 'S'ESCLOP' are
written in faint yellow paint on the
rock — not easily seen at first.
*(Note: this landmark is easily missed
on the way back; you might like to
leave something additional here as a
marker.)*
Now *carefully* follow the cairn-
marked way across this lovely
open plain (at times it's hard to
spot some of the cairns hiding
among the rocks and tall clumps of
pampas grass). To the left you can
now see the long high western
slopes of Galatzó — very
impressive from here, and about
15 minutes later the plains of
Calvià appear across the valley to
the south. The scenery is beautiful,
and the silence of this wild and

71

rocky basin between the two southwesternmost summits of the Tramuntana sierra is broken only by the cry of a bird, or the echo of a bleating goat.

At **1h25min** the route approaches a few sparse trees, where the rocky path veers south downhill.* The path takes you towards the right, and then descends into a gully, amongst some trees. You really have to look hard for the cairns now, to follow the rocky trail as it rises slightly from the gully and then descends to the right around the head of a valley, among incredibly tall clumps of pampas grass and spiky scrubs. Now a steepish zigzag ascent up a rough overgrown path, waymarked with yellow paint spots, will bring you up to a fairly LEVEL AREA (**2h15min**), where the cairns are well placed and easier to follow. The path becomes earthen and, on the right, there is a BARBED WIRE FENCE (this is where you will join the main route if you went up over the ridge as described in the footnote).

Now you find yourselves on a little prairie, so pretty in spring, when masses of wild flowers exhibit their bright colours. The path veers left, up through a few trees, and eventually comes up to a saddle, the **Coll de Sa Font d'es Quer** (**2h45min**). A large circular area is

---

*It is possible to leave the main path here (by a fairly LARGE CAIRN), and instead of going south on the main route, find a way cross-country up the rocky slope to the right (west). You would rise up to a ridge, the **Serra d'es Pinotells**. Keep left along the tops of this sierra, passing two triangulation points, and then head down a steepish slope alongside a BARBED WIRE FENCE. You rejoin the main route at the bottom, by a cairn, and turn right to continue (see main walk notes after the 2h15min-point). This route, through scrub, is rough but not difficult, and it is slightly shorter. Note, however, that it is *not waymarked* except for a couple of cairns near the double 'summit' of the ridge.

crossed — a good place to picnic, with the huge rocky massif of S'Esclop rising high ahead of you. From this point it is easy to follow the narrow path as it snakes towards the mountain. Just over the col, and looking down to the left, you can see the ruins of an old stone dwelling. Some 10 minutes along, ignore a path forking down to the right (it leads to the Font d'es Quer, a mountain spring inside an old mine, and then makes a steep descent through the cleft of the Quer torrent down onto the Ma-10). Since your aim today is the great *mola* of S'Esclop, keep ahead at this point — making for an old stone wall that rises up the slope of the mountain.

Here you can take your pick: you can either round the mountain or follow the main walk up to the summit.

To round the mountain, take the narrow path sloping down to the right (some 100m/yds before a METAL SIGN up on the stone wall). This path completely rounds the

northwest slope of S'Esclop just below the rocky summit, with stunning panoramic views down over the westernmost part of the island. This route takes about an hour; the path is not easy to distinguish, but small cairns mark the way. You come up to the far western slope and round the end of the *mola*. From here there are no paths, but the long rocky southern slope can be descended without much difficulty. Then bear left back down towards the path above the ruined hut, completing the CIRCUIT OF S'Esclop in about 1h30min.

To climb to the summit, keep left along vaguely-trodden goat tracks, following sporadic cairns which lead along the only really viable route up the steep rocky cliff. You come up to the SUMMIT RIDGE at **3h50min**. Another few minutes towards the left will bring you to the southwest end of the *mola*, the SUMMIT OF S'Esclop (926m/3037ft). Just beyond the summit are the ruins of a stone shelter where François Aragó, a Frenchman, lived a solitary existence at the beginning of the 1800s while working on a triangulation point to measure the meridian. If visibility is good, you'll want to remain up here, taking in all the marvellous panoramas that surround you. It is spectacular atop this long and lonely rocky ridge, surrounded by a deserted wilderness, with 'civilisation' stretching out far below you.

Return now to the point of descent and come back down to the **Coll de Sa Font d'es Quer**. From here, follow the same route back to your car, taking note of your marker to descend to **Son Fortuny**. You reach the MA-10 AT KM97 after a tiring but exciting day's hike of about **6-7h**.

See also photograph page 13
Distance/time: 7.5km/4.7mi; 3h
Grade: easy, with gentle ascents of under 180m/600ft
Equipment: stout walking shoes, sunhat, picnic, water, insect repellent; windproof in cold weather
How to get there and return:
🚌 to/from Santa Eugènia. Coming from Palma on the Ma-3040, turn into the second road on the right (by Bar Ca'n Topa) and then take the first left: there is plenty of good parking in the shade on this wide road. Or by 🚐 (Timetable 2); ask to be put off at 'Ses Coves'. The return bus leaves Santa Eugènia from the stop on the corner of Carrer S'Estació. Note: The only convenient buses are on Sundays and holidays.

Short walk: Puig de Santa Eugènia. 4.5km/2.8mi; 1h30min; easy, with ascents of only about 80m/260ft. Equipment/access as main walk (but bus times are convenient any day of the week). Follow the main walk as far as the GATES TO THE **Puig d'en Marron** (45min) and then pick up the notes again at the 2h10min-point. This avoids the ascent up the Puig d'en Marron, but still takes in the wonderful panoramic views from the cross monument.

This delightful country walk is beautiful at any time of year. The Puig d'en Marron is draped in a thick blanket of evergreen pine forests, and the hills are riddled with caves containing silent memories of a Moorish past.

Start out in **Santa Eugènia** by walking back to the MAIN ROAD (Ma-3040) from your car, and turn left to walk out of the village as far as the turning up left signposted 'SES COVES' (**20min**). (Start the walk here if you come by bus, deducting 20min from the following times.) Now turn up this pretty country lane, following it round to the left a few minutes later. Keep straight ahead where a tarmac spur turns off right to the square, by the picturesque old stone houses of **Ses Coves** (**30min**), privileged with far-

reaching views across the plain. Follow the lane as it winds down away from the houses, passing a CAVE on the left with an old WINE-PRESS in it (photograph overleaf). A wooden door just to the right of the wine-press (now overgrown and jammed shut) opens into a huge cool cave where wine vats were once stored.

The lane twists to the right, widens by an old WELL, and narrows again. On coming to a fork (**40min**), go left through a little valley, dotted with cottages amidst orange groves and flowering fields. You will reach the GATED ENTRANCE TO THE **Puig d'en Marron**, on the right, at **45min**. This is usually locked, but there is an access gap to the left of the gate, and so your gentle climb to the top now begins. In spring the beautiful song of the nightingale can be heard echoing in the pine-scented silence; you may spot a variety of other birds and see little rabbits scurrying away into the bushes as your footsteps disturb their peace. Looking to the right after the first bend in the track, you can see other caves on the soft sandstone hillside across the valley.

At **1h05min** the route divides into two earthen tracks. The continuing one goes through the woods between weekend cottages and descends the hill on the south side, to the Camí de Ses Olleries, where you could turn left back to Santa Eugènia. But take the right-hand turn, to follow the main track. Keep right at each fork for about another 15 minutes, after which you will leave the woods and come out onto the OPEN PLATEAU which covers the wide brow of the hill. From here, to your right, there is an excellent view towards the north, including the coastline on clear days.

Bear left across the open fields towards the elevated TRIANGU-LATION POINT (320m/1050ft; **1h25min**), which is somewhat obscured by trees. Continue beyond it, along a narrow path, to come to a wide clearing with a stone wall on the right, from where there are some good views down over Palma Bay and the airport runways. To explore a bit, go right, through the gap in the wall, and follow a narrow trail which veers right and then left (leave a marker here for the way back). In only two minutes the trail descends to the long-abandoned **Ermita de Son Seguí**, a hermitage where monks lived from the 1600s up to the 1820s. There are still orange groves in its walled-in gardens … together with an old well and three wooden crosses by the entrance to a cave.) To return, retrace your steps back down the mountain, as far as the gated entrance to the *puig*. Back in the valley (**2h10min**), turn sharp right (the opposite direction from which you came), to continue along the lane. Set back above on

Flowering fields at Santa Eugènia

The old wine press near Ses Coves (left) and the cross monument atop the Puig de Santa Eugènia (Picnic 7)

because the path comes up from this lovely little valley, but once through, the stillness is left behind, as winds whipping across the plain catch at your clothing. Now climb the low stone wall to the left, to make your way up to the cross monument atop the **Puig de Santa Eugènia** (245m/804ft; **2h30min**). What a magnificent view! The extensive Tramuntana sierra stretches across a wide horizon, with the plain below and many towns and villages dotted about like a multicoloured patchwork quilt (Picnic 7, photograph page 13.

To end the walk, go back down over the stone wall, and head down left past a gnarled old pine, through scrub, to a walled-in stony track. At the bottom, turn right and then left, down the steep rough tarmac. You come into **Santa Eugènia's** MAIN SQUARE at **3h**. Head straight downhill and take the second right to find your car.

the hillside, a huge mound of large boulders marks the site of an ancient MOORISH BURIAL GROUND. Continue uphill now and, after about 150m/yds, turn left downhill at a fork, passing the gated, arched entrance to an old well. Just after this, turn left again, down what looks like the access path to a house. When the path ends at a drystone wall, look carefully: a faint red paint spot marks the beginning of a narrow path up the hillside. In only about five minutes you rise up to a ROCKY PASS (before climbing up through the pass, be sure to take a look back at the view to the south). I call this the 'Shangri-La Pass',

8 SANTA EUGÈNIA • SO NA ROSSA • SENCELLES

Map begins opposite and ends below; see also photograph pages 74-75

Distance/time: 7km/4.3mi; 1h40min

Grade: easy, almost level walk along tarmac lanes

Equipment: good walking shoes, sunhat, water, picnic (optional); windproof in cold weather.

How to get there and return:
🚌 to Santa Eugènia (Timetable 2); return by 🚌 from Sencelles (Timetable 2)

Short walk: Santa Eugènia — So Na Rossa — Santa Eugènia. 6km/3.7mi; 1h20min; easy. Equipment as main walk. Access: 🚗 to Santa Eugènia; park by the orchard, as described below. Follow the main walk to So Na Rossa and return the same way.

This is another very pretty country walk based on Santa Eugènia. It's at its best in spring (it is too exposed for a hot summer's day, but viable most of the year). While it is ideal for beginners, I would recommended it to anyone. It winds gently up and down along a ridge, with wonderful vistas across to the Tramuntana mountain range. Just past the old hamlet of So Na Rossa, the view down over the small village of Biniali below the ridge is very picturesque.

Start the walk in **Santa Eugènia** (see map opposite): walk out of the village towards ALGAIDA along the main road (Carrer S'Aljub; Ma-3100). At the end of the village turn left into a lane, opposite an orchard and a METAL SIGN, 'KM7'. (Some electricity lines cross the road near here.) If you have come by car (Short walk), drive this far and turn *right* into

the wide lane opposite. Drive past the orchard fence and park well tucked in; then walk back, cross the main road, and take the lane to Sencelles.

Now it's really easy! Ignore any left or right turns, just follow the lane all the way to Sencelles. Soon after starting out, you'll see some picturesque windmills on the low hill to your left and, as the hill

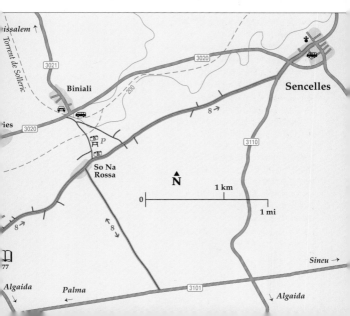

Above: approaching Sencelles;
left: So Na Rossa

sheep bells carries on the breeze. (The walk can be extended here, if you have time to spare, by taking the lane on the right for about another half hour and returning to this point.)

To continue to Sencelles, keep ahead. When the lane bends to the right (**50min**) and another narrower lane leads down left to BINIALI (Picnic 8), there is a splendid view down over the plain across to the mountain range.

Continue following the lane along the ridge, passing wooded areas and open countryside, small pretty cottages and bigger Mallorcan manor houses. Eventually coming out onto the SENCELLES/ALGAIDA ROAD, turn left for Sencelles. At the junction, cross over carefully and keep straight ahead until you reach the village square in **Sencelles** (**1h40min**), where you can find refreshments at the bar while waiting for your bus.

begins to fall away, the distant mountain range on a blue horizon comes into view. Hopefully the weather is still and clear.

Keep straight ahead at a crossroads (**25min**); you are now well into the countryside, surrounded by open fields dotted with small cottages, and bordered on both sides by blackberry bushes, wild asparagus shrubs spiking out of the stone walls and — if it's spring — a multitude of wild gladioli, poppies, daisies and the beautiful blue flowers of the borage plants.

Come to the ancient hamlet of **So Na Rossa** at **40min**, where it seems time has stood still for centuries; grass grows outside the front doors, and the tinkling of

9 VALLDEMOSSA • MIRADOR DE SES PUNTES • CAMI DE S'ARXIDUC • PUIG D'ES TEIX • COMA D'ES CAIRATS • VALLDEMOSSA

See also photographs pages 22, 52, 56 (top), 83

Distance/time: 14km/8.7mi; 6h30min

Grade: strenuous, with ascents totalling some 800m/2625ft. The high, mist-prone trail of the Camí de S'Arxiduc is only suitable for those who are sure-footed and have a head for heights and only in good weather conditions *(not recommended in high winds)*.

Equipment: hiking boots, sunhat, water, picnic, whistle, compass, extra rations; windproof and extra clothing in winter

How to get there and return: 🚌 to/from Valldemossa (Timetable 8), or 🚗 (three large paying car parks on the main road from Palma, opposite the row of cafés)

Short walks: both are strenuous; equipment/access as above

1 **Valldemossa — Mirador de Ses Puntes — Coll de S'Estret de Son Gallard — Valldemossa.** 7km/4.3mi; 3h30min; a climb and descent of about 450m/1475ft. Follow the main walk to the 2h15min-point, then turn down right, back to Es Pouet. From here go left to retrace your steps to Valldemossa.

2 **Valldemossa — IBANAT shelter — Valldemossa.** 6km/3.7mi; 2h30min; a climb and descent of about 350m/1150ft. Follow the main walk to Son Gual, and walk straight ahead (to the right of the house), through a residential area. Turn left on a wide jeep track 15 minutes later (signposted 'REFUGI' further up) and follow it past the **Font d'es Polls** (Picnic 9) to the SHELTER. This walk can be extended to include the climb to the Teix peak (add another 300m/1000ft; 2h).

O ne of the island's best walks, boasting both splendid views and historical interest. Moreover, it offers so many permutations that anyone with energy can tackle a suitable part of the walk. The main route climbs the thickly pine-wooded mountains near Valldemossa to a fabulous view-point, skirts the edge of a high plateau on the Camí de S'Arxiduc, scrambles up to the Teix peak, and then returns to Valldemossa through the pretty Cairats Valley.

Start the walk from the BUS STOP or CAR PARK in **Valldemossa**: walk back up the main road towards PALMA, making for the large old HOUSE WITH A SQUARE TOWER (Son Gual) up above the road on the left. Pass all the car parks, go left up the road by the pedestrian crossing, take the first right, then turn left just *before* the front of **Son Gual**. *(But for Short walk 2 keep straight ahead past the house.)* Take the next right fork, coming up to a HIGH STONE WALL. Turn left here, and then curve round to the right, to find a wide track at the top of the road (the Carrer dels Olives), leading off into the gorse scrubs. Follow it uphill for a few minutes, beside the fence, and turn left up a rocky path. A further five minutes uphill, having past one or two disused woodcutters' trails, go over the wooden LADDER-STILE at the gate. Turn sharp right uphill on the next bend (red arrow), to follow the wide but stony woodcutters' trail that zigzags fairly steeply up through the woods. (A narrow earthen path up right, immediately past the ladder-stile, cuts off the

Lichen-coated holm oaks (Quercus ilex) *testify to the dampness in the woodlands (top); old bread-baking oven near a sitja (middle) and the Es Pouet spring (bottom). Opposite: the Camí de S'Arxiduc, at the edge of the plateau*

first bend.) Rise to a DRYSTONE WALL (**1h**) and you go through the gateway. *(Turn sharp right now, if you are doing Walk 10b.)* Just beyond the gateway you come onto level ground — an extensive shaded area, perfect for taking a breather.

From here keep straight ahead through the trees (where vague paths fork off to the right), cross a *sitja,* and come to a wide clearing with an old well — **Es Pouet** ('little well' in Mallorcan, but the water is not drinkable). Here there are paths going off at various angles. If you wish to shorten the walk by omitting the ascent to the Mirador de Ses Puntes, take the path off right here: it leads directly up to the Coll de S'Estret de Son Gallard and from there up onto the plateau *(Walk 10c takes this route).* The main route keeps

80

straight ahead (north), and then veers left, to wind up the wooded slopes to the **Mirador de Ses Puntes** (**1h25min**), from where there are superb views down over the coast — if swirling mists don't tease you. *Take extra care here;* parts of the surrounding wall have crumbled away.

Returning from the *mirador,* fork left almost immediately (some 30m/yds from the viewpoint). You are now on the famous **Camí de S'Arxiduc**, a mountain bridle-way straddling the tops of these peaks and bordering the high plateau, built for the Archduke Luis Salvador of Austria's pleasure. The path (faint at times) ascends gradually and climbs a rocky slope up to a TRIG POINT (856m/2808ft; **1h45min**). It then continues through the woods, where lichen-covered branches testify to frequent mists. At **1h55min** you arrive at the ruins of a STONE SHELTER atop a rocky peak (867m/2845ft) and enjoy your first view down over Sa Foradada, the rock pierced with a hole jutting into the sea below Son Marroig, the archduke's main mansion (photographs pages 86 and 87).

Go carefully down the rocky slope now, and keep on the descending path through the trees, to come to the **Coll de S'Estret de Son Gallard** (**2h15min**), a mountain crossroads. A path off right here leads back to Es Pouet, and on the left a path (closed to walkers and not shown on the map) leads down to the Ma-10. Our route lies straight ahead. Beyond a rest area with stone seats, the rocky path becomes steeper and, after going

through a gap in an old stone wall, comes up through the last of the trees to join a stone-laid trail; here turn left, to zigzag up onto the high plateau. Once at the top, the views are magnificent! To the west, Galatzó (Walks 3-5) thrusts its peak through scudding clouds, and the high pine-covered mountains of Planici rise up from the valley; below you lies Sa Foradada on a long stretch of rugged coastline; to the south, Palma's huge round bay glistens like a mirror, bordered by the high cliffs of Cap Blanc (Walk 32), with the isle of Cabrera on a hazy horizon. But this stone-laid trail skirts the edge of a high plateau, with very precipitous drops to the left; be *extra vigilant* along here if it happens to be misty or windy! At about **2h50min** a large cairn to the left of the trail marks the be-

ginning of the steep descent down the **Cingles de Son Rul·lan** *(Walk 10c),* and five minutes later you come to the **Puig Caragolí** (944m/ 3096ft), a rocky elevation rising off the plateau. An engraved stone plaque dated 1990, homage by all mountaineers to the archduke, can be seen at the top. This makes an excellent picnic spot: there are magnificent views of the highest peaks, the Puig Major and the double-peaked Massanella (Walk 23) to the northeast, with the impressive ridge of the Teix closing off the southern horizon. A few minutes further along, a small group of pines provides welcome shelter on a hot day. This area is known as **Fontanelles (3h)**. *(Walk 10b rejoins the main route here.)* Now the path becomes earthen and veers left, to come to another,

larger group of pines; this is also a good picnic spot on days when it is too hot at Caragolí — especially if you go off the path to the right to find a cave and water-hole. Back on the main route, wind up over another rocky rise and along to a viewpoint over Deià, then turn right to curl down round the head of the valley. Here, on the wide bend (just before the trails begins to descend), you will come to the signposted turn-off to Es Teix. Scramble up to the SUMMIT OF Es Teix (1064m/3490ft), for more never-to-be-forgotten views, then return to this point — allowing an hour up and back. Rejoining the main route, now descend into the beautiful **Cairats Valley**, passing by the remains of a *casa de neu* (snow pit). Shortly after, you join a wide track and come to the IBANAT HIKERS' SHELTER (**5h30min**). Behind it is a covered open area, with a fireplace and stone seats. A little further

82

down the steep track, you pass the picnic area of **Sa Font d'es Polls**, a mountain spring surrounded by poplars (Picnic 9). From here, a rough path leads off left up onto the Serra d'es Cairats (signposted), from where it is possible for energetic mountain walkers to climb to the summit of the Teix (*Walk 10a descends this path*). From the Poplars' Well onwards, several of the now-extinct Mallorcan industries (see pages 52-57) can be visited. At **6h** go through a gateway and keep straight ahead, going through a second gateway further on. Where the track ends, fork right onto the tarmac and a little later curve down left to **Son Gual**, to return to the BUS STOP/CAR PARK in the centre of **Valldemossa** (**6h30min**).

10 THREE VARIATIONS ON THE TEIX CIRCUIT

Map opposite; see also photos
pages 22, 52, 56 (top), 80, 81
**Walk a: Serra dels Cairats:
circuit from Valldemossa.**
12km/7.4mi; 4h30min; fairly
strenuous, with ascents totalling
about 650m/ 2130ft. Equipment
and access as Walk 9
**Walk b: Fontanelles: circuit
from Valldemossa.** 11.5km/
7.1mi; 5h; strenuous, with ascents
totalling some 800m/2625ft.
Equipment and access as Walk 9;
*see notes on page 80 about the Camí
de S'Arxiduc.*
**Walk c: Valldemossa — Cingles
de Son Rul-lan — Deià.** 11.5km/
7.1mi; 4h30min; strenuous, with
a climb of about 550m/1800ft and
a steep descent of about 650m/

*On the high plateau, just before the
descent of Les Cingles de Son Rul-lan*

2130ft. You must-be sure-footed
and have a head for heights.
Equipment and access as Walk 9;
return by 🚌 from Deià (Timetable 8). *See notes on page 80 about
the Camí de S'Arxiduc.*

While Walk 9 is the classic circuit to the Teix, these
challenging routes not only offer new perspectives
from the heights, but provide those based at Deià or
Valldemossa with more scope for exploration.

Walk a: Follow Short walk 9-2
up to the **Teix.** From the summit,
walk down southwest along the
top of the cliff (well cairned at the
outset). Bear left, away from the
cliff-edge, alongside an old stone
wall with a fence on the top. Look
out for a red-painted number on a
stone, and climb over the wall
here. Soon the way is well cairned
again, and a wide zigzag path leads
you straight down the cliffs of the
Serra d'es Cairats to the **Font
d'es Polls** picnic area. Continue
down the track to **Valldemossa.**
Walk b: Follow Walk 9 to the 1h-
point and go through the gateway
in the stone wall. Now turn sharp
right, to follow the trail up to a
fabulous *VIEWPOINT* on the right
over Valldemossa (some 20min
up, not long after a bend to the
left; Picnic 10). Continue ahead;
you join Walk 9 in 2h, by a clump
of pines (this area is called '**Fontanelles**'). Turn right to follow
Walk 9 from the 3h-point. (Or

turn left and use the map to follow
the Walk 9 in reverse — to the
Coll de S'Estret de Son Gallard or
the Mirador de ses Puntes — and
then back down to **Valldemossa**.)
Walk c: Follow Walk 9 to **Es
Pouet.** Turn right, up to the **Coll
de Son Gallard,** right again up
onto the **Camí,** and right again.
At a large *CAIRN* (the **2h50min-**
point in Walk 9) turn left down a
well-cairned path. It hugs the face
of the cliffs before descending
through trees. Some 55min from
the top, turn sharp right, to pass a
well-preserved bread oven and
cross a *sitja.* Go through a gap in a
wall and rise to a wider trail, with
open views over Deià. The trail
makes a U-turn to the right just
before some rusty gates near **Son
Rul-lan.** Still following the cairns,
you descend ancient cobbles and
then a narrow zigzag path. At a
track just below a farmhouse, turn
right to descend past the Hotel Es
Molí and onto the Ma-10 in **Deià.**

83

Distance/time: 4km/2.5mi; 1h30min
Grade: quite easy, with a descent/ascent of some 200m/650ft
Equipment: stout shoes, sunhat, swimwear, towel, suncream and plastic shoes in summer, picnic, water; windproof in winter
How to get there and return: 🚌 or 🚐 (Timetable 8) to/from Deià

Alternative walk: Deià — Cala de Deià — Lluc-Alcari. 3.5km/2.2mi; 1h50min; grade as main walk, but you must be sure-footed and have a head for heights. The coastal path is eroded in places *(potentially dangerous)*. Equipment and access as main walk; return by 🚐 from Lluc-Alcari (Timetable 8). See notes opposite.

The combination of sea air and mountain landscapes makes all walks around Deià irresistible. This short hike, one of my three main walks based on the village, is an easy walk for beginners, or a relaxing day for the more energetic. You'll sample stunning coastal views and have time to swim — either at the Cala de Deià or at one of the more secluded coves visited on the Alternative walk.

Start the walk in **Deià**: go down the STONE STEPS OPPOSITE THE OLD WASH-HOUSE (on a bend in the main Ma-10 road, by the side of a stream). Keep downhill, ignoring all offshoots. Pass by the Archaeological Museum, veering left and then down right along the main lane (one or two more lanes join from the left). Where the tarmac ends keep straight ahead: take stone steps past the side of a house (sign: 'TO THE BEACH. A LA CALA'). The deep bed of the **Torrent d'es Salt** is on your right. Climb a STILE (**15min**) and, a couple of minutes further down, bear right — where 'CALA' is painted in white at

ground level. Climb a second STILE (**20min**), then follow a beautiful stone-laid path. At **25min** join a tarmac road and turn down left, to a wide parking area. At **35min** you come to the picturesque little pebbly beach at Deià Cove (**Cala de Deià**). Here you will also find a terraced restaurant perched up on the rocks above the beach, from where you can take good photographs of the cove. Swim in the clear cool waters if it's summer, or enjoy the fresh salt winds blowing white foam up onto the rocks on a winter's day.

Before turning back, head *above* the cove for more fine views: take the *second* set of stone steps up to the left, to climb the side of the cliff. Five minutes further along (**40min**), take the steep earthen path down to the left *(care is needed here; the fencing has broken away)*. Now you have a beautiful view of the cove framed between pines. *(The Alternative walk carries on from here to Lluc-Alcari.)* Return to the cove and retrace your steps up to the WASH-HOUSE (**1h30min**) — or follow the twisting tarmac lane (with short-cuts) up into **Deià** village at KM61.2 on the Ma-10 (BUS STOP).

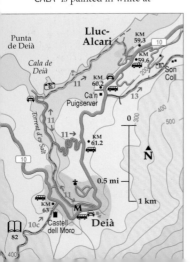

Deià

Alternative walk

Follow the main walk to the **40min**-point. At the bottom of the earthen path, a few metres before a little house, turn up right (small CAIRN), and rise up to the next terrace (small CAIRN), where you veer left to find the coastal path. A little further on, the path becomes well marked with red paint spots, and continues along the coast — at times very near the edge of the cliffs. There is some danger of vertigo at **45min** and beyond.

You will come to some stone steps leading down to the water at a point where the path crosses some fallen rocks. *Extra care* is needed here, as the path slopes directly down to the sea. There is a fixed rope to help you make your way down the rocks. Just below here, you will find an excellent place to swim (on calm days) from a STONE PLATFORM. (The rocks here are full of sea urchins, hence my suggestion of plastic shoes.)

The path continues up through a beautiful wide grassy terrace, complete with stone table and seats for picnicking, then narrows again, veering right, round the rocky cliff-edge. Climb TWO STILES (**1h05min**, **1h07min**) and at **1h10min** bear left (the right-hand path ascends to the Hotel Ca'n Costa below Lluc-Alcari). A few minutes more bring you to another well-shaded area with a ROUND STONE TABLE AND SEATS. Continue over the stone wall (you may see '57' painted in red on the rock), to find some stone steps down to a rocky platform and bathing area. (You could end this walk here with a swim and then return to Cala de Deià.)

To continue, follow the path past a stone-walled enclosure and climb some steps. At **1h25min** come to a high stone wall surrounding a house (below are two more excellent beaches — one of them popular with naturists).

Turn up right here,* to climb steps and then a path up to Lluc-Alcari, keeping right at a fork halfway up and passing through an iron gate near the top. You reach the picturesque, bougainvillea-covered houses at the hamlet of **Lluc-Alcari** in **1h40min**. Turn up left, to meet the Ma-10 at the KM59.6 marker (**1h50min**). There is a BUS STOP nearby.

*There is also a path and steps from the other side of the house, which lead to the same place.

Map on reverse of the touring map; photos on pages 27, 110
Distance/time: 16.5km/10.2mi; 5h15min
Grade: Strenuous, with an ascent/descent of 680m. The walk follows tracks and paths as far as Puig Galileu, then runs pathless along the Galileu ridge; although it is marked by cairns, it is only suitable for experienced route-finders.
Equipment: hiking boots, sunhat, water, picnic, windproof, compass
How to get there and return: 🚌 (Timetable 3) or 🚗 to Lluc
Shorter walks (access and equipment as main walk):
1 Lluc to Puig Galileu and back. 13.5km/8.4mi; 4h40min. Grade, as main walk, but there are no potential route-finding problems. Follow the main walk to Puig Galileu and return same way. This version omits the ridge walk, yet takes in the stunning views.
2 Lluc — Ses Voltes — Casa de neu — Lluc 11.2km/7mi; 4h.

Fairly strenuous, with an ascent/descent of 600m/1965ft. Follow the main walk to the GR signposts at the 2h05min-point. Keep ahead here, coming to the snow pit (Casa de Neu) two minutes later. Return same way. This version avoids the climb to summit, but still offers some excellent views.
Alternative walk: Lluc — Puig Galileu — Pas de Ses Cases de Neu — Coll d'es Prat — Lluc. 13km/8mi; 6h. Strenuous, with an ascent/descent of 720m/2360ft. Follow the main walk to the **Pas de Ses Cases de Neu** and keep right, to descend into the valley (15min). Veer west and climb gently to the **Coll d'es Telègraf** (25min). Now turn left (south) and zigzag up past a snow pit and through a gap in a wall. Eventually you reach the **Coll d'es Prat** (55min), from where you can pick up Walk 22 (at the 2h 45min-point) to return to Lluc.

An ancient trail built in the late 1600s from Lluc Monastery up the steep northern slopes of Puig Galileu (1181m) was an amazing feat of engineering. It fell into disuse, but has recently been restored. It climbs gently at first, then steeply in cobbled sharp bends up to one of the most exciting vantage points from which to contemplate the jagged double peak of Massanella and Puig Major from the north. The main walk then traverses the pathless (but cairn-marked) *carena* (ridge) of Galileu — enjoying a bird's-eye view down over the lakes/ But you can simply enjoy the terrific panorama from the top and return the same way. Another alternative is to walk down southwest from the pass between the double summit of Galileu and link up with the route coming down from the Coll d'es Prat (Walk 22), which you can follow back to Lluc.

The walk begins at **Lluc Monastery**: walk towards the **Font Coberta** spring at the far end of the large car park, where you'll see the GR221 signpost 'VOLTES D'EN GALILEU'. Go up the stony steps, and soon wind up out of the Lluc valley through holm oak woods

and wild olive trees, following the wooden posts.Shortly after passing a double *sitja*, keep ahead, rising up to the MAIN MA-10 ROAD (**30min**). (Just before the road there is an ideal picnic spot just off right by a *sitja*). Cross the road, passing another GR221 SIGNPOST, and continue gently up a wide track. Soon (**45min**) some wooden posts point the way, eventually through a gap in an old stone wall (beware of a low wire at head level!). Follow more posts, joining a wider track; a couple of minutes later passing a picnic spot with table and bench up in the trees by another *sitja*. Keep uphill, guided by the wooden posts.

At a level area you come to the start of the cobbled **Voltes d'en Galileu** (Galileu Bends; **1h 15min**). Just below, off to the right, you can see the remains of a *casa de neu* (snow pit) down below the signpost. Here we start to zigzag up the steep cliff, the start also of some wonderful panoramic views, always improving, over the Lluc Valley, Puig Roig, Tomir, and many more landmarks.

After rounding the head of a steep scree, you come up to the top of the Voltes (**2h**), and five minutes later reach more GR signposts: COLL DE SES CASES DE NEU. FONT D'ES PRAT. Two minutes straight ahead there is a SNOW PIT and the ruins of an old stone HUT where the snow-collectors lived, on a patch of flat ground ideal for picnicking (lovely in spring!) under the shelter of the long rocky ridge. *(Shorter walk 2 turns back here.)*

To continue the main walk, go left at the signposts, to follow a narrow rocky path which rises gently to the **Pas de Ses Cases de Neu** (**2h15min**). From the pass, do *not* follow the path where it curves to the right over the pass. Instead, take the narrow rocky continuing path and follow this down to a small flattish area, with the peak of Galileu immediately ahead of you. Some cairns indicate the best route, straight up the spine of the rocky slope. From the top of **Puig Galileu** (1181m; **2h30min**) the panorama is simply stunning: the jagged peaks of Massanella's north face are very close by to the south, Puig Major looms up behind the Serra dels Teixos, you see the incredible gash of the Torrent de Paréis, Puig Roig, Tomir, Alcúdia Bay, the plain, and even Menorca on a clear day — a 360° swoop of the island.

Return to the **Pas de Ses Cases de Neu**, and keep straight ahead up the opposite slope to rise onto the long rocky ridge; this part of the walk, pathless but cairn-marked, should only be followed by experienced mountain walkers and on a clear day. Follow the cairns carefully, eventually coming up to the higher of Galileu's two peaks (1182m), with wonderful views all the way. Keeping to the contours of the ridge, you will be able to see the snow pit where Shorter walk 2 turned back down to the right; it's on your return route. *Beware* of a WATER-HOLE at about **3h***, and keep along the tops, with Puig Major in front of you. The ridge descends gently, veering north, until you come to the point, on a rocky rise (**3h20min**), from where you can see the blue waters of the Gorg Blau (this section is not very well cairned).

Return from this viewpoint and, by following the natural decline and the odd large cairn (now below the ridge) in an easterly direction, descend to a flattish area with pampas grass. Soon more cairns appear, indicating the way down a cleft in the rocks. Eventually you arrive at the ruined STONE HUT and SNOW PIT (**3h50min**). Return down the **Voltes**, back to **Lluc** (**5h15min**).

---

*It's possible to shorten the ridge walk from this point, by turning down to the right and following cairns back to the snow pit.

See also photograph page 97
Distance: 8km/5mi; 2h35min
Grade: easy, after an initial ascent of some 180m/590ft
Equipment: stout walking shoes, suncream, sunhat, picnic; warm clothing and windproof in cold weather
How to get there and return: 🚌 or 🚐 (Timetable 8); get off the bus or park east of Deià, near Ca'n Puigserver (the KM60.2 marker on the Ma-10). Motorists can return by taking a bus back to your car (Timetable 8).

Shorter walk: Font de Ses Mentides. 4.5km/2.8mi; 1h30min. Grade/ access as main walk. Follow the main walk to just past **Son Coll** hamlet, and go left at the bottom of the wide stone steps to the SPRING; return same way.

This walk follows a very picturesque route through the mountains down into the pretty Sóller valley. After sampling the panoramic sea views, the fresh mountain air, and the splendid descent into Sóller, I'm sure you will want to discover more of Mallorca on foot.

Begin the walk in **Deià** at KM60.2 ON THE MA-10. Walk up the slope opposite the wide gates of **Ca'n Puigserver**. Walk up the steep track for just under five minutes and then (soon after a bend to the right and opposite a house) turn left, up a rocky path marked by a cairn. You are now on the old wayfarers' route from Deià to Sóller, extensively used before the Ma-10 was built. Keep ahead on the easily-followed path, and soon you will begin to get some excellent coastal views — do turn to admire them from time to time. At about **30min** come to a little cluster of houses known as **Son Coll**; the trail passes between them. Five minutes later, you can make a short detour to visit the **Font de Ses Mentides** (Picnic 13), a mountain spring with a small stone seat: go left at the bottom of the wide stone steps, and descend some rather more ancient steps for a couple of minutes to find it.

Back on the main route, cross over a tarmac lane and continue ahead. Go through a gateway, after which the path descends gently through the woods, gradually veering away from the coast. If you're walking here in spring, you will see violets,

scarlet pimpernel, clematis, daisies, wild orchids, wild gladioli, and many other plants common only to the Balearics. Go through a couple more gates (at the second one there is a signpost back to Deià), and continue down onto a wider track, where you veer right, coming down to a wide gate. Go through, coming immediately onto the front patio of **Son Mico** (**1h30min**), a large old Mallorcan mansion, now converted into a rural tourism property. You can visit the interior of this huge house, full of antique farming implements. And while you're here, why not sample some freshly-squeezed orange juice, or some home-made Mallorcan sweetcakes or pastries?

Then continue ahead, past the front of the house and down some ancient cobbled steps, from the top of which there is a lovely view

Sóller tram (above) and the lovely woodland path from Ca'n Puigserver

down over the Sóller basin, with the high mountains rising in the background. You pass a pretty 13th-century CHAPEL, now almost completely in ruins. Take the narrow path directly in front of the chapel doorway, and walk alongside drystone walling. Later, when the way widens, keep ahead, with lovely olive groves below. The route is now quite obvious, turning left further down, and then right (where the words 'SOLLER' and 'DEIA' are engraved in the stone wall). Later you descend some wide stony steps. (At the top of these steps, there is an old rusty sign nailed to a tree on the left, and a wide track heads off left just here — it leads to an excellent picnic spot on a pine-shaded grassy mound after some 20m/yds.)

At **2h** you will have your first impressive views of the beautiful Sóller valley, surrounded by the island's highest peaks — including the Puig Major, the triangular summit of L'Ofre, and the Serra d'Alfabia. A few minutes later, you cross above the 'wild-west' mountain railway, just above a tunnel. The path descends gradually into the valley, becoming a wide track further down.

At the tall square house standing on its own on a corner, turn down left, and come out onto the MAIN SOLLER/PALMA ROAD almost opposite the PETROL STATION (**2h30min**). If you are taking the bus back, go left down the main road, then take the first right after the petrol station. This brings you to the Plaça América (see Sóller plan on page 95) and the bus stop. Alternatively, walk into **Sóller** centre, and head right uphill to the RAILWAY STATION (**2h35min**).

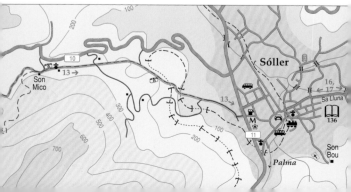

See also photos on pages 12, 57
Distance/time: 7km/4.3mi; 2h30min
Grade: fairly easy, with some steepish slopes near the beginning. Outward climb of 300m/985ft.
Equipment: hiking boots or strong shoes, water, picnic, sunhat; windproof in cold weather
How to get there and return: 🚌 to KM11.9 on the Alaró/Orient road; there is room to park several cars at various points nearby, or park in Orient village, and walk back to the starting point (1.5km).
Short walk: Orient — Es Pouet — Orient. 4.5km/2.8mi; 1h20min. You avoid the final ascent to the castle (100m/330ft), but still enjoy superb views. Follow the walk to the 45min-point and return the same way.
Alternative walk: Alaró — Es Verger — Es Pouet — Castell d'Alaró — Alaró. 15km/9.3mi; 5h30min; grade and equipment as main walk. Access/return: 🚌 to/from Alaró (departure times page 131). Walk up the main street in Alaró, turning right at the

top on the Carrer Sollerich. Some 500m/yds after leaving the village, turn left up a tarmac lane sign-posted 'Es Pouet/Castillo'. Why not walk up in the afternoon, spend the night at the lodge, and carry on with Walk 15 to Santa Maria the next day? Good Mallorcan food can be had at the hikers' lodge (tel: 971-182112 for overnight stays), or at the Es Verger restaurant half-way up.
Note: Once at the Castell d'Alaró, you may be able to explore the **Arab water tanks** shown on page 57 or the mysterious **Cova de Sant Antoni**. These paths are shown on the walking map but not highlighted in colour, since (just at press date) the landowners closed the mountaintop off to walkers. Alaró town council is negotiating to keep the land open. On your arrival at the top, enquire at the hikers' lodge to see if you have access. A full description of the paths is on page 92 (and note that you would need a *torch and rope* to visit the cave).

Т he once-magnificent Castell d'Alaró was so impregnable a fortress that an Arab commander-in-chief was able to hold out for almost two years after the Reconquest of Mallorca by Jaime I in 1229. Much of its old wall still stands, defiantly resisting ruin, blending reluctantly with the sheer reddish escarpments, thousands of feet above the plain.

Start the walk AT KM11.9 ON THE ALARO/ORIENT ROAD, opposite the farm of **Son Bernadás**. Go up through the access gate on the left (facing Orient), and veer left round a large water tank, to walk through terraces planted with olive trees. In **3min** you'll see 'CASTILLO' painted on a rock at ground level; keep ahead. After **10min** the path begins its steep zigzag climb through the woods. At **30min** you will come to an ideal picnic spot — a grassy outcrop to the right of the path (Picnic 14; this is also an

excellent vantage point from which to photograph the Orient Valley). A little further up, go through an old gateway, giving access to a little clearing. This is also a good picnic spot if you prefer the shade, but there are no views. The path continues up to the right, and comes up to a wide track (**40min**). Turn up right here and, almost immediately, you will find yourself in a large clearing on the col known as **Es Pouet** (**45min**). You may be surprised to see cars parked here! It is possible

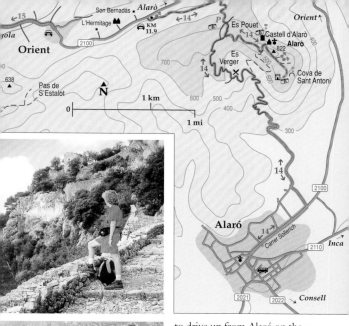

to drive up from Alaró on the other side of the mountain, but is not recommended for hire cars or nervous motorists! You may also come across some donkeys, the amiable transport 'vehicles' waiting to be laden with provisions when the jeep arrives from a shopping trip down on the plain. They appreciate a pat on the muzzle.

Cross this clearing to the stone wall at the top, and find the beginning of the centuries-old STONE-LAID TRAIL on your left (signposted). Soon the awesome escarpments of the **Puig d'Alaró** loom up ahead, as the trail becomes a series of stone steps winding ever higher towards the top. In **1h10min** go through the imposing archways and the entrance to the **Castell d'Alaró**, to come onto a flatter, grassy, wooded area, from where the

Stone-laid steps below the Castell d'Alaró (top), the donkeys appreciate a pat on the muzzle (middle), and rock-climbers on the walls of the Puig d'Alaró (bottom)

91

views are superb. On the left lies the incredibly beautiful and unspoilt valley of Sollerich, with its backcloth of high mountains, the peaks of L'Ofre (Walks 16 and 20) and Massanella (Walk 23), and many others. To the right, the wide sweep of the plain reaches down as far as Palma and its huge circular bay. *Extra care* is needed near the unprotected precipitous drop on the left! It is wiser to admire the view to the north from a little further uphill, where there is a protecting wall. Then continue up to the HIKERS' LODGE and the little pilgrims' CHAPEL (**1h20min**).

Intrepid, sure-footed walkers may like to enquire at the lodge about access to the Cova de Sant Antoni. This diversion will take 1h, and *do not enter the cave without a torch and a rope* (there is an iron rope-hold at the entrance). The route down to the cave begins at the far end of the hikers' lodge: go through the metal gate by the side of some old latrines and follow the cairns, bearing right after five minutes. You descend the wooded slope towards the edge of the bluff. When you reach the old WATCHTOWER *(caution needed if you go inside)*, turn left for about 20m/yds, to find a small hole in the rock. It doesn't seem to lead anywhere … until you crouch down inside, and shine your torch to the right, to find the hidden entrance to the **Cova de Sant Antoni**. If you have no rope, do *not* try to enter it: its dank floor, slippery with moss, slopes straight to the edge of the precipice! Content yourself with some good photos from the entrance. If you *are* carrying a rope and venture in, you will find a water tank fed by a small mountain spring near the top of the cave, as well as some beautiful stalactites.

If you don't have a head for heights, and prefer safer walking, just visit the ARAB WATER TANKS *(algibes)* shown on page 57 (middle): go through the metal gate by the latrines, and fork left in about three minutes. Another few minutes down and you're there. Take care at the steep drop beyond the lowest tank.

Return the same way to KM11.9 ON THE ALARO/ORIENT ROAD (**2h30min** — or 3h30min, if you visited the cave).

The Puig d'Alaró (left) and the Puig S'Alcanada frame the entrance to the Orient Valley

15 FROM ORIENT TO SANTA MARIA

See photograph on page 12
Distance/time: 14.5km/9mi; 5h
Grade: easy, gentle descent all the
way (except for an ascent of some
160m/525ft about 35min into the
walk). Thick undergrowth can
obscure the path in places.
Equipment: hiking boots or stout
walking shoes, long-sleeved shirt
and long trousers, insect repellent,
sunhat, suncream, water, picnic,
whistle, compass; windproof in
winter
How to get there: 🚗 private
transport (taxi/friends) to Orient
To return: 🚌 (Timetable 10) or
🚌 (Timetable 6) from Santa
Maria
Note: An impressive cavern lies en
route, the Avenc de Son Pou. It is
one of the largest on Mallorca,
perhaps second only to the 'Cam-
pana', a cave near the Torrent de
Pareis large enough to hold
Palma's cathedral! Because of
damage to stalactites, it is kept
locked and may only be visited
with a guide. For details, contact
the Santa María town hall (tel:
971 620131, *Mon-Fri only*), as
visiting days tend to change. If
you visit, you will need a **torch**!

This lovely walk starts from the magical mountain village
of Orient, set in a green and fertile valley untouched as
yet by mass tourism, although frequently visited by hikers.
Why not climb the stone steps up to the quiet little square by
the churchyard before beginning your walk today? It's very
picturesque.

Start out at **Orient**: walk along
the quiet country lane towards
BUNYOLA for just over **20min**,
then turn down a wide earthen
track on the left (the second one
you come to, just where the road
begins to climb in bends). Go over
the wooden LADDER-STILE and
continue along a walled-in track.
Climb another LADDER-STILE over a
gate (**35min**), and cross the
stream bed further down — on
stepping stones if water is flowing,
to find some WOODEN SIGNPOSTS
on the left.
Before continuing up the opposite
slope, make a short descent to see
one of Mallorca's impressive (if it
has rained recently) waterfalls —
the Salt d'es Freu. To get there, go
straight down the walled-in track
at the left of the stream bed. This
descends in long zigzags for about
10 minutes and, just where it
passes between rock walls (on a
bend to the right), you come to
the high cascase of the **Salt d'es
Freu** (**45min**), where the rushing
waters of the Freu stream tumble

noisily down over the rocks —
very impressive when flowing, but
also beautiful in dry weather,
when you can explore *(carefully)*
over the huge green moss-covered
boulders.
Back up at the signposts, begin to
zigzag to the right up the hillside
and, at the top, continue straight
ahead. When you come to an
arrow marker (**1h20min**) turn
sharp right as indicated, cross a
sitja, pass a LIMEKILN, and continue
ahead, gently descending. Some
25 minutes lower down, the path
narrows quite a bit, and runs high
above the east bank of the gorge,
where the **Torrent d'Es Freu**
flows through a wild and beautiful
landscape. Continue over a ROCKY
PASS (**1h50min**), the ideal place
for a drink stop or snack, perched
up on the karst rocks in the shade
of pines, high above the gorge,
with lovely views down over the
torrent as it travels south through
thickly wooded slopes.
After this, the rocky path descends
abruptly, delving deeper into the

93

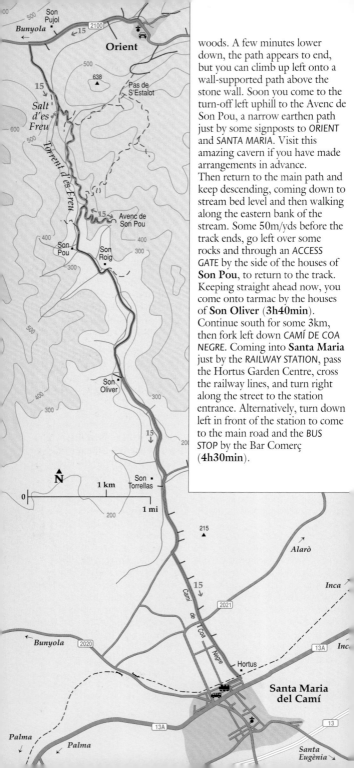

woods. A few minutes lower down, the path appears to end, but you can climb up left onto a wall-supported path above the stone wall. Soon you come to the turn-off left uphill to the Avenc de Son Pou, a narrow earthen path just by some signposts to *ORIENT* and *SANTA MARIA*. Visit this amazing cavern if you have made arrangements in advance.

Then return to the main path and keep descending, coming down to stream bed level and then walking along the eastern bank of the stream. Some 50m/yds before the track ends, go left over some rocks and through an *ACCESS GATE* by the side of the houses of **Son Pou**, to return to the track. Keeping straight ahead now, you come onto tarmac by the houses of **Son Oliver** (**3h40min**). Continue south for some 3km, then fork left down *CAMÍ DE COA NEGRE*. Coming into **Santa Maria** just by the *RAILWAY STATION*, pass the Hortus Garden Centre, cross the railway lines, and turn right along the street to the station entrance. Alternatively, turn down left in front of the station to come to the main road and the *BUS STOP* by the Bar Comerç (**4h30min**).

16 SOLLER • BINIARAIX • ES BARRANC • ES CORNADORS • L'OFRE • SOLLER

See map on reverse of touring map; see also photographs pages 97, 98, 104

Distance/time: 16km/9.9mi; 8h30min

Grade: very long and strenuous, but not technically difficult; ascent/ descent of about 1150m/3775ft. The ascent of L'Ofre is steep and rocky.

Equipment: hiking boots, water, picnic, sunhat, windproof

How to get there and return: 🚂 (Timetable 11), 🚌 (Timetables 8, 9) to/from Sóller. Or 🚌 to/from Biniaraix and start at the 35min-point.

Alternative walks

1 Cúber Lake — Sóller. 12km/7.4mi; 4h30min; easy ascent (130m/425ft); long descent (600m/1970ft). Sóller/Pollença 🚌 (Timetable 9; *note restricted service*) to KM34 on the Ma-10. Follow the track from the Cúber Lake to **L'Ofre** farm, then turn right downhill for 'SOLLER', to descend **Es Barranc**. Return: 🚂 or 🚌 as above.

2 The three peaks circuit. 11.5km/7.1mi; 6h; strenuous, on rough, rocky paths. Ascents/ descents of 580m/1900ft overall. Sporadically waymarked with cairns, but a good sense of direction is essential. Access as Alternative walk 1 above; return the same way. Follow the track to the **Cúber DAM**. Just before it (by an electricity substation), take a track downhill. This narrows to a path and crosses a stream. Above a wall, turn right, to climb a rough path to **Sa Rateta** (1084m). Head west along the ridge, descend to a col and bear left up a rocky path to **Na Franquesa** (1060m). Again head west, descend to another col, then make a third, final ascent — to **L'Ofre** (1091m). After 'bagging' three peaks over 1000m, return to the col below L'Ofre and turn left. Then bear right at a fork, heading northeast below Na Franquesa. Turn right on the track down to the lake and return via the DAM to KM34 (or round the north side of the lake).

Certainly a tough ascent, but worth every minute! And although this classic walk can no longer be a circuit (due the closure of the footpath at S'Arrom Farm), it is still one of the best-loved hikes on Mallorca. The Camí d'es Barranc

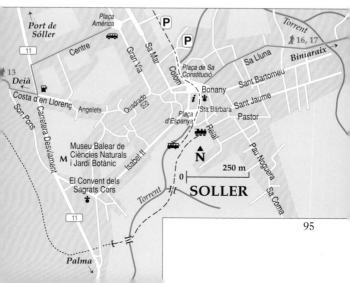

95

offers a fair bit of shade at the outset, but later you're mostly in full sun. The route is idyllic when the stream is in full flow, with water cascading over huge boulders and down the falls. After a period of drought the stream dries up, as much of the flow seeps underground through the porous limestone and only surfaces after heavy rain. Nearing the top of the ravine, the exhausting ascent is soon forgotten, as more and more panoramic views open up all around.

The walk begins in the Plaça de Sa Constitució in **Sóller**. Take the narrow CARRER DE SA LLUNA and keep straight on for 'BINIARAIX' (signposted). The lane eventually crosses a bridge and comes into the picturesque little square in **Biniaraix** (**35min**), dominated by a large plane tree. Keep on in the same direction, along the CARRER SANT JOSEP (a sign on the wall says 'LLUC A PIE') and, a minute later, turn right to make your way up the signposted **Camí d'es Barranc** (Picnic 16).

Cross a small BRIDGE at **45min**, the first of several, and continue gradually ascending this beautiful stone-laid trail, the mystical music of a rushing stream echoing in the ravine. Some 10 minutes up the *camí*, where the way levels out briefly, ignore a walled-in path to the right. (*Walk 17 turns right here.*) Keep up the main route, below the impressive cliff-face above you on the right, and soon cross a SECOND BRIDGE over this curious stream, which occasionally disappears underground, so that one moment you can hear the water cascading over the rocks, and then all of a sudden you notice how silent it is. On the ascent, you will pass several old stone houses, once used by the olive pickers, and also many inviting rock pools. There are a couple of water taps along the route, too; don't worry about the 'fizzy' appearance of the water, just let it settle before you drink it. Cross a THIRD BRIDGE at **1h45min** and, soon after, a

FOURTH BRIDGE. You'll pass a large house with a very neat stone wall; turn around and see how high the olive terraces reach!

At about **2h** turn sharp left with the main path. (The level path ahead leads to the stream bed by a ruined lime kiln, beyond which an impressive waterfall cascades into a rock pool. Walk 17 comes in here, from the far side of the stream bed.) As you proceed, the views become more and more scintillating — Sóller seems so far away now; you just have to keep stopping to look back down the ravine and across the Sóller basin … as well as to catch your breath. The stony trail passes below another fantastic cliff-face at about **2h30min** and, further along, as you round a bend, a rugged deep ravine appears below on the right, with the far-away sound of a rushing torrent coming up on the echo.

Not long after, you come to the iron gates that guard the **Finca de L'Ofre**. There are various signs: 'Private property', etc, but you *are* allowed access here. Please make sure you close the gate behind you. The path now levels out and rounds the head of the canyon. At **3h** a sign on the right, 'MIRADOR D'EN QUESADA', indicates your onward path — down to the right, across a little BRIDGE (or walk the plank if it's been washed away!). Beyond the bridge, the narrow earthen path soon starts to climb in earnest; this is an ascent in full sun on a good day. Take a

The 16th-century church of Sant Bartomeu in Sóller

breather now and then, to turn and admire this beautiful high valley, with the L'Ofre farmhouse hiding below in the trees, the impressive triangular peak of the L'Ofre mountain (1091m/3575ft) rising in the northeast, and the wild and silent Serra d'Alfabia south of the valley.

Keep on up, passing two unusual rock formations in the form of columns, and in **3h30min** reach the pass between the two 'horns' of **Es Cornadors**, where the path divides. Turn right, up past the shelter, and scramble over the brow of the mountain, down to the precarious **Mirador d'en Quesada**. The views are truly breathtaking! The entire Sóller valley lies below you like a miniature toy world. Beyond lies the bay with its lighthouse, and all around you a magnificent panorama of the island's highest peaks — L'Ofre, the Puig Mayor, Massanella, the Serra d'Alfabia, the Teix…

Either picnic here, or back at the shelter, which offers some shade. Then return to where the path divides, this time going left, retracing your steps back down to the LITTLE BRIDGE (**4h**).

From here follow signs to 'L'OFRE' — the triangular pine-wooded peak you have been admiring from the viewpoint. The signposted route heads up the main track and then through the trees, soon coming up to a wide track just below the col. Just off to the left there is a viewpoint over the Sóller basin (with a broken telescope). *(The Alternative walk and Walk 20 descend this track.)*

Carry on another couple of minutes up to the **Coll de L'Ofre** (**4h35min**), for a sweeping view down to the lakes. Then walk back down to the track off left which rounds the base of L'Ofre*, picking up the notes for Walk 20 at the 1h50min-point (page 104) to climb to the SUMMIT OF **L'Ofre** (**5h25min**).

From here retrace your steps to the BRIDGE (**6h40min**) and descend **Es Barranc**, to return to **Sóller** (**8h30min**).

---

*Or take the track that starts in the trees just above it. This higher track leads straight up to the col between L'Ofre and Na Franquesa, where you turn right up the long cairned slope to the summit. This approach is slightly longer, but more gentle.

17 ES BARRANC CIRCUIT

See map on reverse of touring map and plan of Sóller on page 95; see also photograph page 97
Distance/time: 6.5km/4mi; 3h
Grade: not technically difficult, but a fairly strenuous ascent/descent of about 350m/1150ft.

Equipment: hiking boots, water, picnic, sunhat, windproof
How to get there and return: 🚂 (Timetable 11), 🚌 (Timetables 8, 9) to/from Sóller. Or 🚗 to/from Biniaraix and start at the 35min-point in Walk 16.

On this hike you'll climb a little-used ancient trail above Es Barranc, on the opposite side of the stream from the famous 'Camí'. You'll go over a col south of three towering sandstone pillars, then descend and cross the stream, to follow the well-trodden Camí d'es Barranc back down to Biniaraix.

Begin in **Sóller**: follow WALK 16 (page 95) to **Biniaraix** and start up the **Camí d'es Barranc**. Ten minutes up the *camí*, where the path levels out, turn right up a narrow, walled-in path opposite an olive tree (there is a CAIRN on top of the wall). At the end, go left through a wide METAL GATE.

You are now on a very old trail, mostly unused by walkers, and privileged with many more far-reaching views than its sister trail below. It climbs in zigzags high above the ravine (watch carefully for cairns, to avoid taking one of the confusing offshoots up onto olive terraces). Soon you can see hikers going up and down the *camí* far below you. Cross a small scree, and continue up, always veering left, and go left at the fork below a terrace. The way is fairly steep and stony, but very exciting. Soon you will come up and over a pass south of THREE SANDSTONE ROCK PILLARS only visible from the Camí d'es Barranc. This wide rocky brow makes an excellent picnic spot with magnificent views. There is a little house down the slope, but it's private property.

To return, follow the path over the brow and downhill, coming into the trees where the path crosses the stream bed (just below an impressive waterfall after heavy rains). Turn left by the ruined LIME KILN, to join the **Camí d'es Barranc**. Look back up to the three pillars on your descent back to **Biniaraix** (**2h25min**), then walk on to **Sóller** (**3h**).

Biniaraix (top), and the Camí d'es Barranc

See map on reverse of touring map; see also photograph page 102

Distance/time: 15km/9.3mi; 6h15min

Grade: moderate, with several ascents and descents; the final stretch from Cala Tuent to Sa Calobra is strenuous and tedious. All good trails and tracks. Longest single ascent: 250m/820ft (Coll de Biniamar)

Equipment: hiking boots or stout walking shoes, water, picnic, sun-hat, insect repellent, swimwear, towel; windproof in cold weather

How to get there: 🚌 (Timetable 11), 🚌 (Timetable 8) or 🚂 to Sóller, then taxi or 🚌 (Timetable 9; *note restricted service*) to the Mirador de Ses Barques (or 🚌 direct from Pollença; Timetable 9 as above)

To return: ⛴ from Sa Calobra (Timetable 13) to Port de Sóller. The boat calls at Cala Tuent some

10 minutes after leaving Sa Calobra *on Saturdays only;* it arrives at Port de Sóller in time to catch the bus to Pollença (Timetable 9) or tram to Sóller for the last train to Palma. *Note:* The boat runs all year round *in good weather* (see 'Weather', page 45), but will not take large groups. If you are more than four or five, opt for the Alternative walk described below.

Short walk: Font de Bálitx. 4km/2.5mi; 1h10min; easy. Equipment: stout shoes, sunhat, water, picnic. Access/return: 🚌 or Sóller/Pollença 🚌 to/from the Mirador de Ses Barques (Timetable 9; *note restricted service*). Follow the main walk to the SPRING and return the same way.

Alternative walk: Sa Costera. 12km/7.4mi; under 5h. Equipment and grade as main walk; access/return as *Short walk*. follow the main walk to the 2h30min-point and return the same way.

The Mirador de Ses Barques is a very scenic spot on the mountain road above Sóller. From a height of over 400m/1300ft, we can take in a magnificent panorama of the village and port below, reflected in the shimmering blue Mediterranean and surrounded by the highest mountains of the sierra. The *mirador* is also well known for its orange juice, freshly-squeezed from the delicious orange groves of the Sóller valley. Why not enjoy a sparkling glass of 'sunshine' before embarking on this hike?

Begin the walk at the **Mirador de Ses Barques**: walk up the steps to the right of the gates (sign-posted). Keep left twice, and then go through a METAL GATE (**10min**). Five minutes later you join a wide track and head right. Approach the old farmstead of **Bálitx de Dalt** (Upper Bálitx), but turn down right through the gateway just below the big house. Now you are in the incredibly beautiful valley of Bálitx, where footpaths wind away over the hills,

and a myriad of silvery-leaved olive trees populate a thousand terraces.

At **30min**, just on a bend to the left, take a stone-laid trail straight down to the **Font de Bálitx** (Picnic 18), a hidden mountain spring; this short cut also avoids a couple of bends in the track. To rejoin the track, turn down left from the spring (the path is a little narrow at the bottom). Continue to the right along the main route, passing the huge abandoned farm

of **Bálitx d'en Mig** (Middle Bálitx; **45min**).

In **1h15min** come to the farm of **Bálitx d'Avall** (Lower Bálitx), where María and Guillermo will welcome you to another fresh orange juice, inside the cool interior of this big old farmhouse. They also sell lovely home-made marmalade, little bags of sun-dried apricots, almonds, *hierbas* (a Mallorcan alcoholic drink made with fresh herbs), and many other tempting things. An overnight stay here, with a Mallorcan cooked supper, bed and breakfast, and the use of a stone swimming pool with a breathtaking view will not break the bank, should you wish to turn this into a two-day adventure, but it is best to telephone beforehand to check they have a room (tel: 971-634240 or mobile 608 631011; the summer months are their 'low season').

From the farm, turn down right and descend the stony trail, to cross the stream bed. Then begin a steepish ascent of some 30 minutes up to the pass. At just under **2h** you will reach the **Coll de Biniamar**, where the way levels out a bit and is also refreshed by a cool sea breeze. Now descend again and, about five minutes later (by a bend to the right), find your path down to Sa Costera, where there is an abandoned house. The path begins through a gateway to the left of the track; it takes about half an hour to get down to the house at **Sa Costera** (**2h30min**). Just looking at the beautiful view down over the bay of **Es Racó de**

Sa Taleca and the shimmering blue waters erases all thoughts of the climb back up from your mind. Find the mountain SPRING hiding in a dark tunnel just up on a ridge behind the house, and enjoy a picnic lunch under the young olive tree.

From Sa Costera, climb back up to the main route (**3h**), then turn down left to follow the coastal route. About halfway to Cala Tuent, watch for a SMALL BLUE ARROW ON A ROCK, indicating a path down to the sea. At the bottom of this path, near the abandoned HYDROELECTRIC PLANT, there's an incredible mountain SPRING gushing out precious water into the sea. Return to the main coastal path. Later, beyond a gap in a wall, keep half left across a clearing, rising slightly across the **Morro d'es Forat**. Meeting a gravel track, follow it down to the left for a couple of minutes, then turn right (sign, 'CALA TUENT'). Five minutes later turn sharp left down a path (red arrow on a tree). The path descends into **Cala Tuent** (**4h30min**), a truly boring place — the only spot of life being the restaurant just above the beach. Just past the restaurant, take the second set of steps down onto the beach, to avoid a long walk round. Cross to the road on the far side, and brace yourself for the long, arduous walk up the tarmac (or wait for the boat if it's Saturday). At the top of the climb you come to the 13th-century chapel of **Sant Llorenç**, from where there is a short-cut path down to the road.

You should reach **Sa Calobra** at about **6h15min**. Relaxing now, on the boat back to Port de Sóller, contemplate the wild and rugged mountainous scenery reflected in the deep blue waters.

19 ES TORRENT DE PAREIS

See map on reverse of touring map
Distance/time: 8km/5mi; 4-6h
Grade: difficult and tough; *only for expert mountain walkers with some climbing experience. For those not used to rock-climbing, it is advisable to take a 20-25m long rope.* **You must be able to swim.**
Equipment: hiking boots, change of clothing in waterproof bag, towel, water, picnic, sunhat, suncream, torch, whistle, windproof, rope
How to get there: 🚂 (Timetable 11), 🚌 (Timetables 8, 9) or 🚗 to Sóller or Port de Sóller, then Sóller/Pollença 🚌 (Timetable 9; *note restricted service*) to the Escorca restaurant at KM25 on the Ma-10 (or 🚌 direct to the restaurant, if coming from Pollença)
To return: ⛴ from Sa Calobra (Timetable 13) to Port de Sóller for connection with ongoing transport (as above).
Short walk: Es Torrent de Pareis from Sa Calobra. Explore the gorge from its mouth (Picnic 19). This is easy but, once at the first high boulders, do *not* attempt to continue without adequate equipment. Take sunhat, swimwear, suncream, wading shoes, water and picnic. Access/return: ⛴ (Timetable 13) or 🚗 to/from Sa Calobra.

Following the course of the Torrent de Pareis gorge is perhaps the island's most spectacular excursion on foot … except for the adventure of its twin gorge, Sa Fosca, where only experts and speleologists dare to penetrate the narrow cascading underground watercourse. Our hike down the Torrent de Pareis, however, is *not* for the inexperienced; you will have to scramble over slippery rocks, wade through icy pools, and maybe even swim — if you venture down here after a rainy period (flash floods are not unknown). In any case this is a walk only for the summer months, May to September.

Start the walk on the WEST SIDE OF THE PARKING AREA opposite the RESTAURANT at **Escorca**. There is a sign here saying the walk takes 5h30min and one must not begin after 12.00. From the parking area descend a few metres, keeping right,until rock blocks the way. Walk between a FENCE and the rock, beneath trees, to the rise, where the path turns sharp left to begin its DESCENT INTO THE GORGE (**15min**). At some rocks further down, turn left again, and then right, following the waymarks; the bottom of the gorge is already visible. Beyond the **Voltes Llargues** ('long bends') you come to a good resting place in the bed of the **Torrent de Lluc** (**1h**). Now follow the stream bed, amongst strewn rocks and boulders, down to the wider **Entreforc** (**1h15min**), where the Torrent de Lluc unites with the waters coming from **Sa Fosca** (the 'Dark Place), to form the **Torrent de Pareis** (the 'twin torrents'). Down here, dwarfed by sheer rock faces and vertical cliffs, the hiker is surrounded by a fantastic wild landscape; the blue of the sky above seems far, far away … and the screech of wild birds and the occasional bleat of a mountain goat echo loudly around the canyon.

Up to here the walk has been quite simple. Anyone who has had problems on this stretch or has not matched these times, *should turn back*, since the next few hours are

101

much more difficult. You will need a good sense of orientation (cairns and paint waymarks are sparse), and clambering over the boulders is extremely strenuous. Remember that if you are in a group, your times will be longer, as only one person can get through the passages at a time.

The path heads uphill to the right for a short way, then goes back into the gorge. The first major obstacle comes up in about 30 minutes. This rock is descended via a chimney-like cleft, below which you come onto a rock area like a giant elephant's back. Two green paint spots indicate where to cross and clamber down. The next obstacle is overcome by taking a path to the left. The final huge rock obstacles have some cables to help: the first on the right, the second on the left. Then the way is easier and passes a cave on the left. From here you walk uphill to the right for a few metres/yards, then go through a cleft in the rock, reaching **Sa Calobra** about 15 minutes later (**4-6h**).

Exploring the lower gorge from Sa Calobra

See map on reverse of touring map; see also photograph page 107

Distance/time: 12km/7.4mi; 5h
Grade: quite easy ascent of 100m/330ft up to the Coll de L'Ofre, but the last 30min stretch (another 200m/650ft) up steep rocky terrain to L'Ofre peak is strenuous.
Equipment: hiking boots, water, picnic, suncream, sunhat; wind-proof in winter.
How to get there and return: Sóller/Pollença 🚌 (Timetable 9; *note restricted service*) or 🚗 to Cúber Lake (KM34 on the Ma-10); park by the lake
Short walk: Circuit of Cúber Lake. 4km/2.5mi; 1h; easy. Equipment: stout shoes, binoculars, water. Access/return as main walk. Follow the main walk to the stream at the far end of the lake,

then fork left, go over a stile and turn back left along the track. Good area for bird watching.
Alternative walk: Cúber Lake— Coll de L'Ofre — Orient Valley overlook — Cúber Lake. 12.5km/7.8mi; 5h. Quite easy ascent of 100m/330ft up to the Coll de L'Ofre; this version cuts out the rough ascent to L'Ofre peak. Access/return and equipment as main walk, but stout walking shoes will suffice. Follow the main walk to the base of L'Ofre mountain (1h50min), then continue along the track for some 15min more, winding down the south side of L'Ofre. You come to a stone house and grassy platform with wonderful vistas across the Orient Valley to the two bluffs shown on page 92 and the plain beyond them. Return the same way.

The L'Ofre peak (1091m/3579ft) is a triangular, pine-wooded mountain with a bare rocky top, boasting some of the most marvellous views up in the Serra de Tramuntana, and it is reached without much effort from our starting point at Cúber Lake. It is also an excellent spot for seeing some of the bigger birds of prey — black vultures, red kites, and eagles … soaring over the still waters or circling high on the thermals between these craggy highest peaks of the sierra.

Start the walk from the small PARKING AREA AT KM34 ON THE MA-10: go through the access gate onto the wide track. Almost immediately, veer off right, to follow the path around the north side of the **Cúber Lake** (Picnic 20). It becomes an earthen track. A few minutes further along, just where logic tells you to keep right, go *left,* to find an elevated, rough track that borders the north side of the lake. Serenity and beauty are just two of the many words one could use to describe the sensation of walking along here beside the water, where occasionally a trout will leap up out of the deep blue

and splash down again, and the far side of the lake reflects the rugged ridge and the peaks of Sa Rateta (1084m3556ft) and Na Franquesa (1067m/3500ft).
At **30min** you pass the FAR END OF THE LAKE; there is a stone refuge with a picnic table just across the water. Soon, cross a small stream and continue ahead along the grassy footpath. *(The Short walk keeps left here.)* You come to the gates of the **L'Ofre** farmlands, where there is a sign requesting that you do not go off the main route.
Go through the ACCESS GATE, and continue along the wide track,

View back to the lakes and the Puig Major (on the left) from the Coll de L'Ofre

which undulates between the high ridges of Sa Rateta and Na Franquesa to the left and the Torrellas to the right. At **1h10min**, after a bend to the left, leave the main track, following red paint spots marking a narrow earthen path up through pretty woodlands. A gradual climb takes you up to the **Coll de L'Ofre** (**1h30min**). Look back here for a spectacular panorama back down over your route through the valley, to Cúber Lake glistening in the distance, with the imposing slopes of the Puig Major in the background.

Continuing along to the right, just past the col, veer off the track for a few minutes and head downhill to the right, for another impressive panoramic view — this time over the Sóller basin. There is even a (broken) telescope. Back on the track, walk downhill for a couple of minutes and then take the track off left,* which rounds the base of L'Ofre. You eventually come to an 'opening', where the track veers round to the left and through a col (**1h50min**). *(The Alternative walk continues straight on down the track here.)* A narrow path to the right leads to another telescope at the

edge of the rocks on the south side of L'Ofre, with sweeping view over the beautiful Orient Valley. On the left, blue and red paint marks indicate the ascent path to the top.

This path soon emerges from the woods and begins its steepish (but not too difficult) ascent up the rocky slope. Arriving on the bare smooth rocks at the SUMMIT OF L'Ofre (**2h20min**), the panorama will astound you! Both lakes are clearly visible far below to the northeast, with the high crags of the Puig Major as a backcloth. Sóller bay and its valley lie at your feet, and many peaks of the Serra de Tramuntana stretch away onto the east and west horizons. The vast plain spreads out to the south, dotted with distant towns and villages. A great reward for not *such* a big effort!

To return, descend to the wide track and retrace your steps to the gates of **L'Ofre** FARM. Then continue straight ahead, rounding the opposite side of the lake and crossing the dam, back to the MA-10 and your transport (**5h**).

---

*Or take the higher track just before it; see footnote page 97.

Map begins on reverse of touring map; ends overleaf; photograph page 111
Distance/time: 16km/10mi; 6h
Grade: quite easy; an ascent of 100m/330ft up to the Col d'es Coloms, then a descent of 650m/2130ft on good trails and tracks
Equipment: hiking boots or stout shoes, water, picnic (but see *Note* about Tossals Verds), suncream, sunhat; windproof in winter
How to get there and return:
Sóller/Pollença 🚌 (Timetable 9; *note restricted service*) to Cúber Lake (KM34 on the Ma-10); return by 🚐 (Timetable 10). If travelling by 🚗, leave the car at Lloseta and take a taxi up to Cúber to start (arrange this beforehand, as there is no taxi rank in Lloseta).
Note: Tossals Verds is a government-run hikers' refuge in a beautiful setting. To spend the night or order a cooked meal *in advance,* log on to www.conselldemallorca.net/mediambient.pedra or telephone 971-173700.
Alternative walks
1 Aumedrá — Cases Velles — Tossals Verds — Aumedrá.
9km/5.6mi; under 4h; moderate, with an ascents/descents of about 500m/1640ft overall. Equipment

as main walk. Access (see map on page 107): 🚗 from Lloseta to Aumedrá. Follow the track from the parking area to **Tossals Verds** (Walk 21 in reverse). Here follow signposting to SA COMA, dropping into a secluded valley. Rise up to the head of the valley to the old farm of **Cases Velles** and turn right on the path near the **Font de Sa Basola** (the main walk route). Now follow this higher path to the right, back to Tossals Verds, and retrace your steps to Aumedrá.
2 Aumedrá — Cúber Lake — Tossals Verds — Aumedrá.
18km/11.2mi; 6h30min; fairly strenuous, with ascents/descents of about 600m/1970ft overall. Equipment as main walk, *plus torch*; access as Alternative walk 1. Follow the track from the parking area up towards Tossals Verds, but go left over a stile before the zigzags up to the refuge. In a few minutes keep right and, further uphill, go through a first TUNNEL. The narrow, rocky path runs through four more tunnels, beside water pipes, and rises (steeply at times) to the **Cúber** DAM. Turn right to the Ma-10, then follow the main walk to **Tossals** and back down to **Aumedrá**.

T his relatively easy, although long walk — one of my favourites — takes you from the heights down towards the plain through ever-changing landscapes — rocky mountain trails, woodlands and streams, craggy gorges and sweeping valleys. For those with energy to spare, the two Alternative walks are ideal circular hikes for motorists.

Start the walk at KM34 ON THE MA-10: walk down the road from the Cúber **Lake** towards the GORG BLAU. Where the water channel (*'Tubería'* on the map) goes under the road, head northeast on the maintenance path alongside it, with the road winding away below, and admire the magnificent views down over the **Gorg Blau** as you contour round the

mountain slopes (Picnic 21). After **50min** or so you come to a BRIDGE signposted 'TOSSALS VERDS'. Cross the bridge, and continue up through the woods on the old cobbled steps (the ancient wayfarers' route from Sóller to Lluc), passing various *sitjas*, remains of the old charcoal industry (see page 55). Soon you reach the **Coll d'es Coloms**

(Pigeons' Pass). Just over the col, ignore the signposted path off right into the woods, towards the rough summit of the Tossals mountain. Continue gently downhill through a dappled landscape of holm oak woods. At **1h05min**, by another signpost to 'TOSSALS VERDS', step down to the right, off the trail, and continue down a shady earthen path. (But first, if you wish to make a 20-minute return detour to the Font d'es Prat, turn sharp left on the main route and use the notes for Walk 22 on page 108, then return to this point.)

The route now takes you through a very pretty landscape of woodlands and streams, and you soon cross a WOODEN BRIDGE over the tinkling waters. A couple of minutes further down, you cross the stream again, this time on large stepping-stones, to continue along a beautiful old rocky trail as it rounds the eastern face of the large craggy Tossals mountain. Where the trail makes a sharp bend down to the left and then to the right, lift your eyes for a minute to look across to the rocky crags opposite, and you will see the old aqueduct which was built to carry the famous **Canaleta de Massanella** (notes pages 54-55 and 109) on its way down to the plain — this is the best view of it. By now panoramic views of the plain have opened up, and the route eventually becomes less rocky. You pass through a gap in an old stone wall and emerge on the slopes of **Sa Basola** where, just uphill from the path, the old WELL of Sa Basola sits on an open incline (**1h45min**). This is a very pretty place in spring, when the field is a mass of high pink asphodels blowing in the breeze.

Refreshed after a drink, continue along the grassy path over the brow of the hill, passing by the ruins of an old farmstead (**Les Cases Velles**) down to the right. Far-reaching vistas ahead show you the distant green fields of the Orient Valley and, to the right, high rocky ridges — from Tossals mountain to the L'Ofre peak. Below you lies a once-farmed, secluded valley (Alternative walk 1), where there are still a few almond trees on the terraced slopes, and drystone walls reach high up the hillside. At **1h55min** ignore a rough path up left off the main path; this little-used route disappears over the brow of the hill.

Continuing along the stony path, you find yourself in a 'rock garden' — all manner of flowering shrubs border the way — bright yellow gorse bushes, wild thyme, wild sage, *Euphorbias* and *Hypericum* throw splashes of colour over the limestone rocks, as you descend ever more gently towards the next valley. Further down, the path begins a more serious descent, twisting and turning through a series of rocky bends, down to the HIKERS' REFUGE OF **Tossals Verds** (**2h20min**). Here you can enjoy your picnic on the grassy terrace where there are a few wooden tables and benches, overlooking the most marvellous view, or eat inside if the weather isn't good. You can buy hot drinks, too, or enjoy a cooked meal if you ordered it beforehand.

To continue on towards the plain, leave the refuge by the large gates and walk down the wide track — a wonderful winding route through a myriad of olive trees on sloping terraces, still surrounded by a mountainous landscape. Further down, the track snakes between the high sides of a very impressive gorge, crosses a boulder-strewn stream via a BRIDGE, and comes down into foothills.

At **3h30min** climb a stile over a

fence at a small parking area at **Aumedrá**, then continue along a tarmac lane. Cross a small bridge and continue through fields and woodlands. It is now fairly level walking, with the stream bed on your left; soon you can see the impressive rocky pine-covered cliffs of S'Alcadena to the right — one of the twin bluffs visible from L'Ofre peak or from the plain (see photograph page 92). Eventually the narrow lane meets the Ma-2110 (THE LLOSETA/ALARO ROAD; **4h45min-5h**) on a wide

bend. Here keep straight ahead, ignoring the first road off left. Eventually turn left into **Lloseta** on the main road, just before the railway bridge. The STATION is just a little further along (**5h30min-6h**).

Cúber Lake (top), with the Puig Major on the far side. Below: the Font d'es Prat de Massanella. The date 1748, engraved down inside the well, is the year in which work on the Canaleta de Massanella began.

22 CUBER LAKE • FONT D'ES PRAT • COLL D'ES PRAT • LLUC

See map on reverse of touring map; see also photographs pages 52 (right), 54, 107, 111
Distance/time: 14km/8.7mi; 4h45min
Grade: strenuous, but not difficult, with an ascent of some 500m/1640ft up to the Coll d'es Prat. Good tracks and paths all the way. The descent to Lluc is easy, but very stony.
Equipment: hiking boots or stout walking shoes, sunhat, water bottle, picnic; windproof in cold weather
How to get there: Sóller/Pollença 🚌 (Timetable 9; *note restricted service*) or 🚗 to the Cúber Lake at KM34 on the Ma-10
To return: 🚌 (Timetable 3) from

Lluc to Palma (or to Inca, to connect with the 🚂 to Palma; Timetable 10), or 🚌 back along the Ma-10 (Timetable 9; *note restricted service*) to your car at Cúber Lake
Short walk: Cúber Lake — Font d'es Prat — Cúber Lake. 6.5km/ 4mi; 2h10min; easy; stout shoes will suffice. Access/return: 🚗 or Sóller/Pollença 🚌 (Timetable 9; *note restricted service*) to/from Cúber Lake. Follow the main walk to the 1h15min-point, then return the same way.
Note: A fee is payable at Comafreda (see *Note* for Walk 23, page 111), but the guard may have left if you pass through in the afternoon.

The tinkling of sheep bells, the wind whispering through the trees, and the gentle music of flowing waters are the only sounds that penetrate the impressive silence of the central mountains of the sierra. The magnificent landscapes change continually, as we admire the Gorg Blau lake (the 'Blue Gorge') from our elevated path alongside the watercourse, walk through the holm oak woods over the 'Pigeons' Pass', and then ascend towards the north face of the Massanella mountain, habitat of great black vultures. This climb takes us through a wilderness of strewn rocks and tall pampas grass towards the highest mountain pass on the island, the Coll d'es Prat (1205m/3952ft): from here, stretching away to the horizon on both sides in a series of high craggy peaks, practically all of the sierra is visible.

Start out BY FOLLOWING WALK 21 (page 105) to the **1h05min**-point, where that walk turns off right for Tossals Verds. Turn sharp left here, down the main route, which becomes much more stony, and go through a gap in the stone wall of the abandoned farm of **Es Prat de Massanella**. Keep straight ahead until you come to a junction of paths: to the right, an overgrown path leads to the famous Canaleta de Massanella ('Note' opposite and pages 54-55), to the left lies

mountain spring of Es Prat, and your route to the col and Massanella lies straight ahead. But first go left to see the **Font d'es Prat** (**1h15min**; Picnic 22), set in a large shady clearing. The crystal-clear waters from inside the well are refreshing to drink, and you can refill your water bottle here for the rest of the journey.
The next stage of the hike begins back at the junction: go over the culvert to find the beginning of the narrow earthen path that leads up

to the Coll d'es Prat (some cairns mark the start). It ascends gently at first, and then becomes steeper, crossing a *sitja* at **1h45min** and passing two more SPRINGS, one with a drinking trough for animals. Stay on the higher of the two paths, which soon emerges from the woods to continue up the long bare slope amongst rocks and high grass. This red earthen path can become a raging torrent in heavy rain! You can now see the saddle up ahead, and at about **2h10min** the path comes up onto the cobbled mountain 'highway', part of the original SOLLER-LLUC TRAIL. From time to time, stop to look back at the magnificent mountain panorama behind you; many peaks are visible, including the Tossals group, Sa Rateta, the triangular peak of L'Ofre, and the Serra d'es Teix on the left.

The route levels out by another stone wall which divides this valley in two. This is the **Coll d'es Prat (2h45min)**. The impressive rocky northern face of Massanella looms up on the right, and you may well see silhouetted hikers up on the peak (Walk 23), the highest accessible point for walkers on the island. And a scan of the skies may well reveal the silent glide of a black vulture or two circling high above you. Go through the gap in the wall, and ... another fabulous panorama unfolds! The huge round massif of the Puig Tomir (Walk 25), surrounded by many other mountain peaks, stretches out below you as far as the rugged northeastern coastline, with the craggy tops of the Cavall Bernat on a distant horizon to your left, and the wide sweep of Alcúdia's bay to your right.

A few minutes further down will bring you to the first of the SNOWHOUSES (*Cases de neu;* see page 52). This one is in fairly

---

Note: From the **Es Prat** farm you may like to take time to see the old **Canaleta de Massanella** (its history is outlined on pages 54-55). The way is overgrown, but keep ahead, with the stream bed on your left. After about 300m/yds, you will come to some pools of water and the beginning of the *canaleta,* now sadly encased in piping. There was a great outcry from conservationists when this national monument was 'modernised' in 1983. It used to be a wonderful adventure to follow the *canaleta* from here when it was free-flowing: one climbed the high stone wall of Es Molinot (the 'big old mill') and had to proceed very carefully along a narrow stretch for about five minutes, as the channel rounded the side of the mountain (see photograph page 54). *If you're not subject to vertigo, and you're sure-footed,* a few minutes along from the wall will bring you far enough to be able to see the arched aqueduct that carries the *canaleta* across a ravine — still a beautiful sight, though overgrown. Although the channel continues round mountains and through tunnels down to Mancor del Valle, about 6km southeast, I would advise you to go no further than the aqueduct.

Lluc: the monastery's mountain setting, courtyard, church with the statue of the Virgin, and one of the black vultures in the aviary

good condition and affords a picnic place sheltered from the strong winds that sometimes blow through the 'funnel' of the high pass. There is also a freshwater SPRING just below.

The route down to Lluc follows this long, winding, rocky trail as it zigzags down into the beautiful Comafreda Valley, where no sound but the tinkle of sheep bells breaks the silence. The path

becomes a track at just over **4h** and later passes below the **Comafreda** farmhouse. Go over the LADDER-STILE at the gate, and wind down left to the LLUC/INCA ROAD (**4h45min**). Go left and over the bridge, to come to the PETROL STATION and roadside café, where you can take refreshments while you wait for the bus to Inca. Or walk on to the Ma-10 for the Sóller/Pollença bus.

Walking beside the water channel (Walk 21), with the Puig de Massanella in the background

Map on reverse of touring map
Distance/time: 10km/6.2mi; 5h
Grade: strenuous, only for experienced mountain walkers. A tough climb of 780m/2560ft over rocky paths (at times not easily seen). You must be sure-footed and have a head for heights; there is a risk of thick mists falling.
Equipment: hiking boots, long trousers, suncream, sunhat, water, picnic, water-purifying tablets, compass, whistle, torch; cardigans and windproof in winter; shorts and T-shirt in summer
How to get there and return:
🚌 to/from Lluc (Timetable 3) or 🚌 to/from Inca (Timetable 10), where you can connect with the same bus. Do not go all the way to Lluc, but ask to be put off at the Lluc petrol station, at the Coll de Sa Bataia. Alternatively, Sóller/Pollença 🚌 (Timetable 9; *note restricted service*): ask for the Lluc petrol station. Or 🚗 to/from the Coll de Sa Bataia on the Ma-2130 (where there is a petrol station); park opposite the café.
Note: Hikers are charged a small fee to pass through the farm of Comafreda, ostensibly to cover costs of litter removal.

The Puig de Massanella is that double-peaked, high rocky mountain in the centre of the Serra de Tramuntana. The second highest mountain in Mallorca, its peaks reach up to 1348m (4421) and 1352m (4435ft). An incredible panorama is seen from the summit — almost all of the island — and, on a clear day, the islands of Menorca and Cabrera are also visible — worth every bit of the effort it takes to reach the top!

The walk begins at LLUC PETROL STATION at the **Coll de Sa Bataia**, south of Lluc. Walk down the Ma-2130/PM213 towards INCA, crossing the narrow BRIDGE. You come to wide iron gates on the right, just past the bend. A stone engraved 'PUIG DE MASSANELLA' lies to the left of the gates, but is often obscured by undergrowth. Go through the access gate, and keep along the wide track as it winds up and veers right (ignore the track straight ahead on the first sharp bend). At **15min**, where two tracks go straight ahead, turn sharp right uphill on an older track, towards the Comafreda farm. After 10 minutes you'll reach a gate; this is where a guard will charge you the fee for passing through the **Comafreda farm**. Just before the track goes through a stone wall (the descent route of Walk 22), turn up sharp left, along a shady earthen track. Now follow the red paint marks; the way becomes more rocky, going through the remains of an old stone wall and crossing a *sitja*. Make sure you follow the red paint marks; they eventually bring you up onto the main track again at about **40min**. Turn up left and follow this wide track through the woods, coming up to the **Pas de N'Arbona** (832m/2730ft) at **55min**. Here the high rocky crags of the **Puig de N'Alí** (1038m/3408ft) rise above you on the left. There are two large engraved stones with arrows here at the pass: one arrow points straight on towards Mancor, another back to Lluc, and a third up right towards the 'PUIG' (de Massanella). Turn right and follow the red paint spots as they lead you up through the trees, now more steeply. At **1h05min** you'll see a red 'II' painted on a boulder on a bend. Further up, the view begins to attract your attention as the trees thin out, and it is necessary to stop for a breather from time to time to admire the splendid scenery — the plain stretching out down to the southern coastline, the city of Palma with its wide bay, and a hazy horizon hiding the sea. Continue up through sparse trees and clumps of pampas grass; the path has become very rocky indeed! Keep looking for the red spots to guide you. At **1h30min** come to the mountain crossroads of **S'Avenc del Camí**, where there is a small deep pit at the right of the path. (Someone has thoughtfully covered it with a huge rock to avoid accidents.) A few steps further up, another engraved stone indicates two possible ascent routes: straight on to the 'FONT DE S'AVENC' or up right to the summit. Since a circular route is always more interesting, let's do the tour in a clockwise direction, first visiting the spring — a good place to picnic and recuperate energy for the final assault. (It is also easier to follow the route this way round.)

The path to the spring climbs the stony slopes, bearing left at first, and then crosses a treeless expanse of white jagged limestone rocks, bearing slightly right. Watch carefully for the cairns and red paint spots — essential here for keeping to the route. Soon after climbing over higher rocks, you'll come to the **Font de S'Avenc** (**2h**), a marvellous place, just like an Aladdin's Cave! Hidden deep in the mountainside at 1200m/ 3940ft, this spring bubbles fresh, cool filtered water all year round. It is best visited in spring and early summer, near midday, when the sun is overhead and its rays illuminate the dark, dank steps that lead down into the mountain (but further down you will need your torch).

An engraved indication stone near the entrance to the spring points the way to the summit, which is only attained after a good deal of clambering over high rocks. One feels so minute on this mountain, nothing more than a speck of humanity, crawling up over the massive moonscaped rock-face like an ant labouring over a boulder. However, at **2h50min** you'll reach the SUMMIT OF THE **Puig de Massanella**! And the panorama is, of course, worth every minute of effort spent — the whole island lies below you, a magical landscape of mountains, hills and valleys. You are now on the highest accessible point on Mallorca, since the summit of the Puig Mayor is out of bounds due to the radar station. In your wonder and admiration, *don't forget to be careful* — just below the summit is one of the island's deepest snow pits (*cases de neu*; see page 52).

To descend, face the plain: you should be able to see a small tableland below, to the left of the peak. Bear left and make your way down over rocks and boulders towards it (if mists are obscuring the view, bear east). Some 20 minutes downhill, it's easy to find the flat earthen path. This winds southeast and then begins a rocky zigzag descent, coming back down to the **Avenc del Camí**. Now follow your outgoing route down to the left, passing **Comafreda**, and coming back down to the **Coll de Sa Bataia** at **5h**.

Map begins on the reverse of the touring map and ends here; see also photographs on page 110

Distance/time: 14km/8.7mi; 6h

Grade: fairly easy, but quite long; ascent of 150m/490ft and descent of 400m/1310ft. Extra care required on the loose, jagged rocks above the stream bed.

Equipment: hiking boots or strong shoes, water, picnic, sunhat, suncream, insect repellent, long trousers, long-sleeved shirt; windproof in cold weather

How to get there: 🚌 to Lluc (Timetable 3) or 🚂 to Inca (Timetable 10), where you can connect with the same bus. Alternatively, Sóller/Pollença 🚌 (Timetable 9; *note restricted service*) to the KM17.4 marker on the Ma-10, at the entrance to Binifaldó and Menut, from where you pick up the main walk just after the 25min-point. If travelling by 🚗, park on the south side of Caimari in time to take the Inca/Lluc bus on the Ma-2140 (Timetable 3) up to Lluc.

To return: 🚌 (Timetable 3) from Caimari — to Inca for the Palma train or for buses to Palma, Pollença or Alcúdia, or to Lluc for the Sóller/Pollença bus. Or pick up your waiting car at Caimari.

Short walk: Caimari — Binibona — Caimari. 5km/3mi; 1h15min; easy; stout shoes will suffice. Access/return: 🚌 to/from Caimari (Timetable 3), or 🚗. From Caimari, follow signposting to **Binibona** (Picnic 24c) along a country lane with far-reaching views, and return the same way.

Relax with a morning coffee at Palma station before boarding your bus to Lluc or train to Inca

Thankfully, there are still some quiet spots in this crazy, stressed-out world of ours, as we shall discover on this walk. From Binifaldó we descend alongside a rocky stream bed, to come onto the beautiful, silent, south side of the Tomir mountain, where some old stone houses while away the time on a grassy plateau high above the plain — a very romantic picnic spot! Later we wind down through thick undergrowth, zigzag down a rocky trail and walk through the lower woodlands to the picturesque little hamlet of Binibona, before following a country lane to Caimari.

Start the walk at **Lluc**, taking the road back out of the monastery. After some 100m/yds, turn left into a wide entrance. Then turn right immediately, along a path past a STONE HOUSE, and go through the gate of the FOOTBALL PITCH and *fronton* court. At the far end you come out onto a wide track. Now follow this track, passing below a CAMP SITE AND PICNIC AREA (Picnic 24b), then winding gently uphill to the Ma-10 (**25min**). Turn left along the road for about 100m/yds, then cross over and follow the rough tarmac lane signposted to 'BINIFALDO' and 'MENUT' (at the KM17.4 MARKER). After a few minutes you will come to two sets of GATES by the forestry station of **Menut**; opt for the left-hand one, using the access gate if this is closed (as it will be at weekends). Follow this lovely woodland lane (Picnic 24d) for a while, passing the big old stone house of **Binifaldó** (**1h**) and continuing uphill in bends to the gates of the Binifaldó WATER-BOTTLING PLANT (**1h15min**). *(The ascent of the Tomir mountain, Walk 25, begins here, to the right of the gates.)*
Go over the steep stone steps at the right of the lower, *wooden* gate, and keep straight downhill on the main track, ignoring the GR way-marking post indicating Lluc off to the right (Alternative walk 25). At **1h30min** the track bends sharply to the right over a double

culvert. Here you have two options: for the first you must be agile, and for the second you must have a head for heights. *Either* continue down the right-hand side of the stream bed and then down the watercouse itself, which even-tually descends a small ravine. Pick up the notes again at the 2h15min-point. *Or* follow the main walk: cross the rocks below the track to pick up the narrow trail which soon begins to ascend through trees. Becoming very rocky, this route rises high above the right-hand bank of the ravine above the bed of the torrent, then descends fairly abruptly over loose rocks, back to the stream bed (**2h15min**).
Now follow a narrower, flatter path from the stream bed through high *Cistus*, being sure to watch for the red paint marks. If you come this way in spring, the strong and fragrant scent of the rock roses and other mountain flora is almost overpowering, while the lazy drone of insects and the song of the nightingale seem only to accentuate the unbelievable peace on this wilder, south side of Tomir. Guided by the red spots, you come to a gap in an old stone wall which marks the boundaries of the **Aucanella** farm (a descent from Tomir's southern slopes joins from the left here). The long-abandoned old stone farmhouse of Aucanella is being restored by a new owner: there should be an

The old farm of Aucanella on the southern slopes of Tomir (before restoration), with the Puig de Massanella in the background

access gate in the fencing, as the descent routes from Tomir and Lluc pass between Aucanella and Aucanaletta to continue down to the plain. However, it is not difficult to continue cross-country in a south-southwesterly direction from the wall, dropping down onto the open fields below the house, until you come to the head of a valley where your rocky descent begins at the end of the last field, by the side of a tree. Here's where you should put on your long trousers, and spread generous amounts of insect repellent over any areas of bare skin to avoid picking up ticks (in hot weather), as you'll find this descending path quite overgrown with tall pampas grass and thick undergrowth.

Further down, the surroundings change, as you go over a rocky pass and zigzag down a long stony trail, finally coming down into the welcome shade of trees and a large clearing. From here, turn right and follow the wide track for about 100m/yds, then turn left down a narrow path (cairn- and paint-marked) through the woods. It soon comes out on the wide track again, where you turn down left

for a short while. Leave the track again, heading right, down another narrow path which takes you into the STREAM BED itself. Follow the rocky stream bed for about 100m (easy boulder-hopping), and soon the path continues off the opposite bank, widening out and passing a WATER TANK. Shortly after, cross the wide stream bed again (cairn-marked) some 100m before a gate. Then follow a wide track undulating through the woods, but turn right just before some beehives, to recross the stream bed. Soon after, you will reach an original gate … made from a bedstead! Go through, close it after you, and walk round to cross another stream.

On coming up to a tarmac lane, turn left and follow it into the quiet little hamlet of **Binibona** (**5h15min**). From the square in front of the houses, turn right and follow the narrow lane straight ahead (the lane down left goes to Moscari), for another half hour, to **Caimari** (**5h45min**). Here turn left, right, left, right, to descend to the MAIN ROAD (MA-2130; **6h**), where you can hail down the bus, or walk to your car.

See map on reverse of the touring map; see also photographs of Lluc on page 110

Distance/time: 12km/7.4mi; 5h30min

Grade: strenuous climb of 600m/ 1970ft. You must be sure-footed and have a head for heights (only recommended for experienced mountain walkers); two screes to be negotiated; risk of falling mists.

Equipment: hiking boots, long trousers, sunhat, suncream, whistle, picnic, water, walking stick, extra clothing; windproof and woollen hat in winter

How to get there and return: 🚌 to/from Lluc (Timetable 3) or 🚍 to/from Inca (Timetable 10), where you can connect with the same bus. Alternatively, Sóller/ Pollença 🚌 (Timetable 9; *note restricted service*) to the KM17.4 marker on the Ma-10, at the entrance to the Binifaldó road (saves 25min). Or 🚗 to/from Lluc, *but note:* on weekdays you can drive to the Binifaldó gates and park there, saving 1h15min *each way*. Use the walking notes below to drive there, but be alert for the water-plant lorries on this narrow lane.

Alternative walk: Lluc — Binifaldó — Lluc. 9km/5.6mi; 3h15min; easy, with an ascent of 220m/720ft. Equipment: stout shoes, sunhat, water, picnic. Access/return: 🚌 or 🚗 to Lluc (see main walk). This lovely route makes an interesting half day circuit. Follow *Walk 26* (page 118) as far as the wide level track at the 1h30min-point, and go right. Pass the house of **Binifaldó** and rise to the gates of the WATER BOTTLING PLANT at the end of the road (**1h50min**), where the main walk goes left to begin the ascent of Tomir. Go over the steep stone steps at the right of the gate straight ahead, then take the GR-waymarked path immediately to the right (Walk 24 continues down the track here). When you meet a wide track (**2h10min**), turn right, over a steep rise; the route levels out in the woods. Go left at a signposted junction, cross some *sitjas,* and then veer right, to go over a stone wall. Now follow the GR signposts to descend towards the Lluc Valley. When you come to the MAIN MA-10 ROAD (**2h55min**), follow it to the right (watching out for the traffic), back to **Lluc** (**3h15min**).

More a mountaineering adventure than a walk, this scramble is only for the sure-footed. Yet anyone can enjoy the pleasant woodland walk along the lane to the foot of Tomir. If the weather is dry, and you're really fit, off we go. The views from Tomir's peak (1103m/3618ft) make the effort well worthwhile — a magnificent panorama of hills, mountains, plains, wide bays and coastline unfolds before you — an eagle's-eye view of Mallorca!

Start the walk from **Lluc**, following the notes for WALK 24 (page 114) to the gates of the **Binifaldó** WATER-BOTTLING PLANT (**1h15min**). *(Here the Alternative walk goes over the stone steps by the side of the wooden gate on the right.)* A sign, 'TOMIR', at the right of the metal gates to the bottling plant, indicates the point where your strenuous route up the mountain begins. Continue along beside the fence for about five minutes, then turn up sharp right, to follow the earthen path up through the trees. It quickly becomes rocky, and before you know it, you are above the tree-line, coming up onto the bare slopes of Tomir. Soon you'll come to the FIRST SCREE AREA, said to be the remains of a glacier; go across carefully and, a few minutes later, cross a SECOND SECTION OF THE SAME SCREE. *Only after you have crossed safely* should you turn

to admire the surrounding landscape: Lluc's valley, the double-peaked Puig de Massanella, the Puig Roig and the Puig Major… Now hike up the steep side of the cliff, to a small rocky PASS, from where Palma is visible on a clear day. Take a breather before climbing the NEXT SCREE. *Extra care is needed here:* do not attempt to climb it in dangerous conditions — just after snowfall or heavy rains, or in high winds, for instance. Further up, the going becomes easier, and the rocky route veers slightly left.

At **1h55min** you will have to clamber up a rock face, with the help of a rope anchored to the rock. Later, the route over the rough terrain becomes less steep; keep watching for the red waymarks and the cairns. You arrive at what appears to be the top at **2h15min**, but really you are just on the long brow of Tomir, and must keep pressing on, bearing left over rocks and rosemary scrubs until you reach the true SUMMIT OF **Puig Tomir** (**2h40min**). *Beware of the very deep snow pit just below it!* Now you have the 'world' at your feet! Take time to admire the breathtaking panorama on all sides before you return the same way to **Lluc** (**5h30min**).

Puig Tomir from the Coll dels Ases near the Puig Roig; this circuit from Lluc (see map) is only open on Sundays and somewhat spoilt by crowds of walkers.

26 FROM LLUC TO POLLENÇA

Map begins on the reverse of the touring map and ends below; see also photographs pages 26, 110
Distance/time: 18km/11.2mi; 6h
Grade: technically easy, but very long. Ascent of 100m/330ft; gentle descent
Equipment: strong comfortable walking shoes or hiking boots, water, picnic, sunhat, suncream; windproof in winter
How to get there: 🚌 to Lluc (Timetable 3) or 🚌 to Inca (Timetable 10), where you can connect with the same bus. Alternatively, Sóller/ Pollença 🚌 (Timetable 9; *note restricted service*) or 🚗 to the IBANAT picnic area at KM16.4 on the Ma-10
To return: 🚌 from Pollença (Timetables 6, 9; *note restricted service on Timetable 9*) back to your base or back to your parked car
Short walk: Lluc — Es Pixarell — Cova dels Morts — Lluc. 4.5km/2.8mi; 2h; easy. Equipment as main walk, plus torch. Access/return as main walk. A very pleasant short circuit with some

excellent panoramic views. Follow the main walk to the **Es Pixarell** CAMPSITE and walk up the rough tarmac track to the Ma-10. Turn right along the road, and take next exit down to the right (a track chained off to traffic). Back in the woods, the track undulates through rocks and trees. After a longish descent offering fine views, take a short detour to the right (opposite some drystone walling): follow the level path through the trees and turn right behind the first rocks. After passing a tree in the middle of the path, turn sharp right to the **Cova dels Morts** (Cave of the Dead) — an ancient burial site. After negotiating some large rocks, the descent into the cave is fairly easy, but you will need your torch. Take extra care in wet weather. Return the same way to the main track, follow it up over the next rise and, when you return to the junction first encountered at the 20min-point, go left, back down the stony steps to **Lluc** (**2h**).

A walk along the ancient Lluc/Pollença route makes a very pleasant change from the rocky mountain trails we've been following in some of the hikes. It is one of the oldest trails on the island and is known to have been a wayfarers' route since the 13th century. The wide track descends gently through beautiful mountainous landscapes, passing below the imposing north face of the Tomir mountain, and offers magnificent vistas of the craggy northeastern coastline and its wide bays.

Start the walk at **Lluc**, taking the road back out of the monastery. After some 100m/yds, turn left into a wide entrance. Then turn

right immediately, along a path past a STONE HOUSE, and go through the gate of the FOOTBALL PITCH and *fronton* court. Then turn

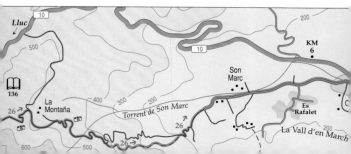

left to cross a WOODEN BRIDGE over a small stream bed and follow the narrow stony steps that snake uphill between boulders and holm oaks. Still cobbled in places, this is part of a centuries-old MOUNTAIN ROUTE BETWEEN LLUC AND POLLENÇA. You rise up onto level ground by a *sitja* (**15min**), where a signpost on the right indicates a short detour to the famous Camel Rock (**Es Camell**). It only takes about five minutes to wind along between the rocks to find this natural limestone sculpture; personally I think it looks much more like a dinosaur.

Back at the *sitja*, continue gently uphill to a JUNCTION (**20min**), where you keep left up the wide, open track. *(The Short walk returns to this junction from the right.)* Just over the rise, a VIEWPOINT WITH STONE SEATS invites you to take a break and admire the splendid view towards the huge massif opposite — the Puig Roig (Red Mountain; 1003m/3290ft), with the Puig Femenias (920m/3018ft) to its right.

The track now descends a couple of bends and soon becomes a very pleasant walk through an 'enchanted wood', passing many weird and wonderful rock formations. Later it winds up to an IBANAT CAMPSITE called Es Pixarell (**40min**), with running water and toilet facilities. From here you enjoy an excellent open vista towards the Puig Major, Mallorca's highest peak. Walk up the rough tarmac lane for a few minutes to the Ma-10, and turn left (caution with oncoming traffic), to find the next IBANAT PICNIC AREA on the other side of

Rock passage near Es Pixarell

the road a few minutes further along. This is also a good place to have a snack, or make use of the facilities.

From the picnic area, go down some stone steps to the right of the WCs and turn left at the bottom, to walk through the trees between more picnic tables and barbecue areas. At the far end, veer slightly to the right: a couple of minutes up the slope will put you on the wide forestry track towards Pollença (it's just beyond the RUSTIC WOODEN GATE that exits onto the Ma-10). Turn right uphill, over the rise, to follow this pleasant woodland walk. The track bends down to the left before heading right again (ignore a wide but faint track off to the right near some poplars). You will come to a small SPRING on a bend (**1h10min**; Picnic 26); turn left

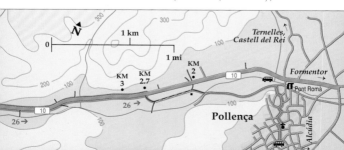

here, passing a STONE REFUGE (can be rented for overnight stays; for information tel: 971 517070). Continue up the trail which now becomes rockier, winding up through the woods for another ten minutes or so, before opening out in more scrubland — with a splendid view towards the huge Tomir mountain rising up directly ahead of you. The route then rises much more gently, to a wide level track (**1h30min**) — another part of the ancient Lluc/ Pollença route. The big house of Binifaldó (Walks 24 and 25) can be seen down to the right.

Turn left here. *(Alternative walk 25 turns right.)* Some 10 minutes later pass through the ACCESS GATE of the *finca* **La Montana**. The route starts to descend and at about **1h50min** you will have your first magnificent view down over the pine-wooded hills and mountains towards Pollença, its port and bay, and the craggy tops of the Cavall Bernat near Cala Sant Vicenç — a beautiful vista, best enjoyed on a clear cool day. And as you continue downhill, the steep scree-covered slopes of Tomir are tremendously impressive looming up on the right at every bend. At the point where the track divides and a left turn leads past the farmhouse (**2h**), go right (there is usually a small cairn in the middle of the right-hand track). The track winds downhill, crosses a culvert over a gushing stream, and joins another track, where you keep right again.

At about **2h25min**, on a bend, a GR WAYMARKING POST indicates your exit off the main track. Turn right, down into thick holm oak woods. Follow this lovely path as
120

Son Marc (top left) and Calvary Hill at Pollença, with the Puig de Maria in the background (above)

it winds down the slopes, and later down some stone steps just above a stream bed. There is a rest area here with stone seats — a lovely place for a pause. The GR waymarks guide you down more wooded slopes and into the **Vall d'en March**, where you join a wide track (**3h40min**). The track is roughly tarmacked at first, but beyond a stretch of faded red 'tiling', the way becomes a wide lane which you follow all the way through the long valley. This last section winds between open fields and farmlands and passes a cluster of lovely old houses at **Son Marc**, across the bridge. The lane finally emerges on the LLUC/POLLENÇA ROAD (MA-10) at a junction (**Las Creus; 4h40min**). With luck you can catch a Sóller/Pollença bus here. If not, walk along the main road for about an hour to the KM2.7 marker, where you turn in right and then go left; a couple of minutes later, keep left along an overgrown path (just where the main track turns right). After passing a house some 10 minutes later, cross the stream bed and turn left along a good road, coming into **Pollença** (**6h**) near the Roman bridge shown on page 26. Head south through the village to the BUS STOP on Marques Destrull (just south of the main square.)

Distance/time: 9km/5.6mi; 5h
Grade: strenuous descents/ascents totalling about 500m/1640ft. Recommended only for experienced mountain walkers; the rough and rocky terrain often makes for difficult route-finding.
Equipment: hiking boots, whistle, sunhat, long trousers, water, picnic; suncream in summer; windproof and warm clothing in winter
How to get there and return: Sóller/Pollença 🚐 (Timetable 9; *note restricted service*) to/from KM10.9 on the Ma-10 (the

Mortitx gates). Alternatively, take a bus to Pollença (Timetable 6) and taxi to/from Mortitx (the taxi rank is near the bus stop); ask driver to return for you no later than 30 minutes before the return bus. Or by 🚗: park by the Mortitx gates (see above), without blocking the entrance.
Alternative: Mortitx Torrent. *Experts* could descend/ascend via the *torrent* (grade and precautions as Walk 19). The blue-waymarked path leaves the track running west from the tennis courts five minutes past a ladder-stile.

A n ancient smugglers' trail, the Camí del Rafal, leads over a wild and savage mountain landscape towards the rugged cliffs of the north coast, where pirates once risked their lives to trade in tobacco and other contraband. The scenery is almost phantasmagoric: huge boulders and wind-sculptured rocks are strewn across an uneven moonscape of ravines, valleys and jagged peaks, creating a vast and lonely wilderness, and the eerie silence, broken only by the shriek of some wild bird, lends an aura of mysticism to this unspoilt and uncivilised part of the sierra. Finally the coastal cliffs are reached, with drops of 200m/650ft to the sea. Their steep escarpments are riddled with huge caves formed by the elements, and ferocious waves beat relentlessly on the rocks below. It's a walk with a difference! And all the more exciting on a wild and windy winter's day.

Start the walk at the main entrance gates to **Mortitx** (or use the access gate a little lower down the road). Go over the CATTLE GRID at the gates, and then go through a second gate, to walk round the TENNIS COURTS. On coming to a small shed on the right, turn right through the GATE. Walk down through the cherry plantations, veering left and then coming up to a locked gate (**10min**). Climb the LADDER-STILE and continue uphill to the right. The track becomes stony now and soon forks: go left. A few minutes further along, begin to look carefully for the beginning of the

Old shepherds' hut at Rafal d'Ariant, with the cliff called 'Es Musclo de ses Cordes' in the background

Es Musclos de ses Cordes Cova de ses Bruixes

Rafal d'Ariant

Torrent de Mortitx

Camí del Rafal

Mortitx

KM 10 Pollença

KM11

Lluc

10

Camí del Rafal to the right of the track (marked by a *LARGE CAIRN*). Looking carefully for the red spots, follow this narrow uneven path downhill until it levels out — now a little vague, but still waymarked. At **40min** you will come to a wall: go through the gate or over the *LADDER-STILE*, and soon you will arrive at the point where the way goes between two huge boulders; climb up between them (on the right-hand side of the cleft, along the sloping side of the rock). The path flattens out again and it becomes a question of very careful trail-finding — be sure to follow the sporadic yellow or red spots and cairns, as the narrow rocky route winds, dips and twists across this rough and empty wilderness. At one point, the way veers left down the right-hand side of some sloping rock (about **1h**). Later it goes right, up a stony slope; here you might like to turn around for a good view of the Puig Tomir to the south, and, if

you can lift your eyes from cairn-searching you might be lucky enough to see some black vultures or a red kite circling overhead. After crossing a flattish area, go over a stone wall and then down the steepish slope on the far side of it, coming down onto the main path. *(This junction is very easily missed on the return; if you miss it, be sure to turn right at the faint junction a little further uphill.)* Soon you will come to where the rough path descends the side of a cliff in erratic bends, from where you will have the magnificent view down over the plain of **Rafal d'Ariant** shown on page 121. You reach the abandoned SHEPHERDS' HUT at about **2h**.

From here it's only a short walk to the cliffs. Find the little path to the right of the house, veering across the flats, and then turn right through a gap in the stone wall; the earth here is a very rusty, almost volcanic colour. This path would take you down to the sea after about 20 minutes, but do *not* go all the way to the bottom. Go only about halfway down (as far as two huge boulders, one at the left of the path and the other slightly lower down), and veer off left here, crossing the stream bed and climbing the rocky slope for a couple of minutes. When you level off, veer right across the sparse scrubs and rocks, eventually coming to a rocky platform some 100m/330ft above the sea. Take *extra care* here at the unprotected drop! To the left you can see a huge hole in the side of the cliff — the **Cova de ses Bruixes** (the 'Witches Cave').

Return to the SHEPHERDS' HUT and then retrace your steps up the cliff. Make sure you turn right at the easily-missed junction, or you'll find yourself in a maze of rock gullies and wilderness! You're back in **Mortitx** in **5h**.

28 THE BOQUER VALLEY

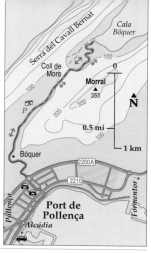

See photograph page 15
Distance/time: 6km/3.7m;
2h30min
Grade: easy — gentle ascents and
descents totalling 160m/525ft
Equipment: stout shoes, sunhat,
suncream, water, picnic, binoculars; swimwear and towel in
summer; windproof in winter
How to get there and return: 🚌
to/from Port de Pollença (Timetables 6, 9; *note restricted service on
Timetable 9*) or 🚗: park on the old
Ma-2210 or just off the
Ma-2200A ring road.

Winter winds, funnelled between the jagged peaks of the
Cavall Bernat and the rocky mountain ridge that
protects the Port of Pollença, howl fiercely through the long
wide Bóquer Valley. And down at the cove, foaming waves
beat upon the rocks… In summer the cove is just a quiet 'pool',
and the valley can be a merciless sun-trap. But the valley has
for decades been a favourite haunt of 'twitchers' who, in any
case, avoid the winter and summer months. Late March to
May and September to October are the best months for bird-
watching. Depending on the season, you might hope to see
stonechats, blue rock thrushes, peregrines, ravens, gold-
finches, crag martins, rock sparrows, black vultures, red kites,
red-legged partridges, booted eagles, serins, Eleonora's falcons, Marmora's warblers, ospreys and Egyptian vultures.

Start the walk on the old PORT DE
POLLENÇA/FORMENTOR ROAD
(Ma-2210). Turn inland just past
the Oro Playa apartments, up a
tree-lined avenue. Go straight over
the ring road roundabout and continue on an earthen track towards
the **Bóquer** FARM, which can be
seen up ahead on the ridge. Go
through the large gates, and walk
past the front of the house
(**25min**), to go through the SMALL
GATE at the end of the courtyard.
Then turn up right, through
another gate, coming into the
Bóquer Valley — silent and
peaceful save for the bleating of
goats. The track winds gently
upwards, through a 'wild west'
ambush scene of rocks and boul-

ders (Picnic 28), then levels out
somewhat. It passes through a
drystone wall and continues on
through the open valley amongst
dotted palm bushes and low rosemary bushes — incredible to think
that you are only just around the
corner from the busy port!
You'll pass one or two fresh-water
SPRINGS, and at about **1h** the path
narrows and descends towards the
cove of **Cala Bóquer**, sadly
littered with picnic remains and
washed-up debris. If the sea is
calm you might swim — or just sit
on the rocks, looking for migratory birds or watching the sleeky
black cormorants dive for fish.
Then return to the PORT the same
way (**2h30min**).

123

29 ERMITA DE LA VICTORIA • PENYA ROTJA • TALAIA D'ALCUDIA • COLL BAIX • MAL PAS

See map page 126
Distance/time: 17km/10.5 mi; 5h
Grade: quite strenuous during the first part of the walk, with ascents of about 400m/1310ft overall; easy thereafter. You must be sure-footed and have a head for heights on the Penya Rotja path. Some rock scrambling involved if you go down to Coll Baix beach.
Equipment: hiking boots or stout walking shoes, water, picnic, sunhat and suncream; windproof in winter; swimwear in summer
How to get there: 🚌 to Alcúdia (Timetables 4, 9) or Port de Pollença (Timetables 6, 9; *note restricted service on Timetable 9*). From either bus stop, taxi to the

Ermita de la Victoria. Or 🚗 to the Ermita de la Victoria.
To return: taxi from Mal Pas to Alcúdia or Port de Pollença for buses, or back to your car at the *ermita*
Short walk: Ermita de la Victoria — Penya Rotja — Ermita de la Victoria.
3.5km/2.2mi; 2h; moderate, with an ascent of 200m/650ft to the Penya Rotja. You must be sure-footed and have a head for heights. Equipment, access/return as main walk. Follow the main walk to the **Penya Rotja** viewpoint and return the same way.

Turquoise, royal blue, pale and deep green — these are just some of the shades of the sea along the beautiful rocky coastline of the Aucanada Peninsula. Contrasting with the deep green of the pines and the sandy-coloured cliffs, this is an artist's paradise of colour. Choose a clear, cool spring day for this walk, when the air sparkles, visibility is good, and a pleasant sea breeze cools the effects of the Mallorcan sun.

The walk begins just above the CAR PARK at the church of the **Ermita de la Victoria**, near the picnic area. (There are some public WCs just up the steps to the right of the church.) Follow the wide track as it climbs quite steeply, with beautiful views down over the Bay of Pollença through the pines — this initial ascent and the fresh salty sea air will soon blow the cobwebs out of your lungs! In about **25min**, just after a sharp bend to the right, look carefully for the beginning of the narrow path to Penya Rotja, leading up left off the main track. *(But for Walk 30, keep on the track.)* This narrow path follows the contours of the **Penya d'es Migdía**. Just below the Penya Rotja (the 'Red Crag'), the path takes you through the 'needle eye' of an ancient WATCHTOWER and ends a couple of

minutes later at a VIEWPOINT with a magnificent outlook to the Formentor Peninsula across the bay and over the colourful Cap d'es Pinar (Cape of Pines) below, surrounded by many-hued coastal waters. This is a lovely place to end the short walk with a picnic. Those not prone to vertigo can enjoy an extra frisson of excitement by climbing to the TOP OF THE **Penya Rotja** (355m/ 1165ft; **1h05min**), where a rusty old cannon has lain silent for the past 400 years; you'll find the beginning of the rocky ascent just behind the stone bunker.
Now retrace your steps back to the main track (**1h40min**), then continue up left, rounding the **Puig de Romaní** and going through a wide barred gateway, after which the track levels off slightly (Picnic 29b). You soon

124

come to a grassy saddle below the rocky cliff of the *talaia*. Now you begin to climb the rocky path in earnest; a slightly exposed feeling may be experienced by some higher up, where little remains of the protective wooden fencing. Soon after rounding the side of the mountain, you come up to the **Talaia d'Alcúdia**, the highest point on the route (**444m/1456ft; 2h15min**). There is a splendid panorama from here: the plain stretches out below, bordered to the north by the impressive Serra de Tramuntana, and you can identify many other landscapes of your island walks — the Puig de Massanella, the Puig Tomir, the headlands of Pollença, the mountains of Artà. Below, the marshlands of S'Albufera glisten in the sun.

A few minutes down from the *talaia,* turn right (by the side of a LARGE CAIRN) along a narrow rocky path which you probably didn't notice on your way up. This long descent soon leaves the *talaia* well behind and crosses the bare slopes of the **Puig d'es Boc**, then descends in zigzags. On one of the first bends, from a high rocky pinnacle, you have the beautiful but vertiginous view of the virgin beach of Coll Baix shown above. After what seems like a thousand bends later, come to a saddle, the **Coll Baix** (**3h15min**; Picnic 29c). Here you'll find another PICNIC SITE, a drinking-water tap, and a small refuge.*

From the picnic site turn right to follow the wide track down through the trees. (*Walk 30 turns right, off the track, after 10 minutes.*) A long but pleasant walk follows, along a narrow tarmac lane through the woodlands of the **Victoria Park**. Go through the

Vertiginous view down to Coll Baix beach (top), and coastal overlook from Penya Rotja

PARK GATES at **4h30min**. Another half hour brings you to the end of the walk at the Bodega del Sol bar, at the **Mal Pas** crossroads (**5h**). From here, it's about another 2km (left), back to Alcúdia — or order a taxi from the bar and enjoy a drink while you wait.

---

*It takes 25 minutes to descend left to the beach. The path may still be hampered by fallen trees, and the last lap involves some clambering over large rocks. *Only swim if it is a very calm day: there is an extremely powerful undertow.* The climb back up is quite strenuous.

125

30 ERMITA DE LA VICTORIA • COLL BAIX • SES FONTANELLES • ERMITA DE LA VICTORIA

See also photograph page 125
Distance/time: 9.5km/6mi;
4h35min
Grade/Equipment: as Walk 29,
page 124
How to get there and return: 🚗
to/from the Ermita de la Victoria
Photograph: Ermita de la Victoria

This fairly long circuit omits the detour to Penya Rotja and allows you to walk back to your parked car at the Ermita de la Victoria via the Coll de ses Fontanelles and over the lower slopes below the Talaia d'Alcúdia.

Start out BY FOLLOWING WALK 29 (page 124). Omitting the deviation to Penya Rotja, continue as far as **Coll Baix** (2h), then turn right, down the wide main track. About 10 minutes later, fork right on a wide track and then walk up onto the right bank of the stream bed (**Torrent de ses Fontanelles**), where a narrow path begins (cairn-marked).

This vague path crosses the stream bed three or four times and eventually climbs to the right up a rocky hillside. When it levels out slightly, look closely for the cairns, to dip down again to cross the stream bed once more. Up the next hillside, the path becomes much easier to distinguish and eventually rises to the **Coll de ses Fontanelles**, a small clearing. From here

enjoy a long but gentle descent (with good views over Pollença Bay). Cross a stream with a small dam and then meet a wider dirt track. Keep ahead on this main track through an OLD GATEWAY. Having ignored all turn-offs, you'll come to a T-junction with another wide track (in woodland; **4h**). Turn up right here, and then *be sure to take the second track to the left*. It eventually narrows into an undulating path and rises steeply to the CAR PARK at the **Ermita de la Victoria** (**4h35min**).

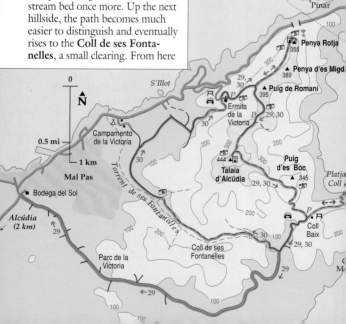

Distance/time: 9km/5.6mi; 3h20min

Grade: easy ups and downs (about 160m/520ft overall)

Equipment: stout shoes, sunhat, suncream, water, picnic; towel and swimwear in summer; windproof in winter

How to get there and return: 🚌 to/from Artà (Timetable 1), then taxi from Artà to Cala Estreta and back. Phone for a taxi from a café (tel: 971-562202), as the taxi rank is not by the bus stop. Ask the taxi driver to return for you 45 minutes before the return bus. Or 🚗 to/from Cala Estreta: leave Artà on the road to Capdepera (Ma-15). Pass the turn-off to Ses Paisses after 0.3km and, 0.8km

further on, turn left at the T-junction, then take the first right (just past the football ground; signposted to 'Cala Torta'). You will follow this *very poorly-surfaced* road for about 10km. Drive through an entrance, and keep left at any forks. After 8km you pass the entrance to an *agroturismo*, a good place to stop on your return. Park well to the side of the road, above the sea, where the road curves back to the south.

Short walk: Cala Estreta — Torre d'Aubarca — Cala Estreta. 3km/2mi; 1h. Easy. No special equipment required, but take ample water on a hot day. Access/return by 🚗. Follow the main walk to the tower and back.

T he salty sea spray splashes over the bare rocks and stings your cheeks as you walk along the deserted headlands of the rugged northeastern coastline on the Artà Peninsula. You'll pass several secluded sandy beaches, far enough away from civilisation to be deserted — even in summer, and the island of Menorca can be seen floating mystically on a hazy blue horizon. Yet there is an air of desolation hanging over these lonely hills — their once thickly-wooded pine slopes ravaged by multiple forest fires over the years have turned this into a bare and lifeless landscape, where only the tougher shrubs and palm bushes eke out an arid existence, and masses of wild chamomile scrubs cover the bare rock slopes. Fortunately there are still some small areas of sea-pine forest along the coast.

The walk begins above **Cala Estreta**, on the left-hand side of the road (as you face the sea). Follow the easily-seen path across

the first inlet and up the other side. Follow the narrow rocky path round the headland, and at **10min** come to a RUSTY GATE at the end of

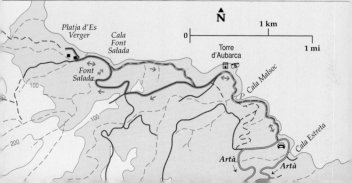

the fence. Go through, being careful on this cliff-edge, and follow the red waymarks around the rugged headland, amongst aromatic spiky chamomile bushes. Soon you'll see the ancient watchtower of Aubarca on the far side of the next bay. Come to beautiful **Cala Malsoc (30min;** Picnic 31), deserted and unspoilt, its wide sandy beach edged by a forest of low sea pines. Swimming here in summer is delightful.

The ongoing path leaves from a sandy recess at the far side of the beach. It rises gradually to the **Torre d'Aubarca (50min),** where the large rocks of the **Faralló d'Aubarca** jut up out of the sea nearby. There are magnificent coastal views from this watch-tower — all along the jagged coastline towards the high cliffs of the Artà mountains.

From the tower take the wide track straight ahead, into the trees. Keep right at a fork, and in **1h** go through a gate. Coming to one or two further forks (**1h20min**), continue straight on, then turn right towards the sea a minute later (where the track bends). You soon arrive at the beach of **Font Salada** (the 'Salty Spring'; **1h35min**). The track circles this beach and later rounds the rocky headland, hugging the coast and passing two solitary tamarind trees braving the sea spray on a windy day. Then you reach the beautiful

long beach of **Es Verger (1h 50min**). In summer its deserted, virgin-white sands and crystal-clear blue waters are very reminiscent of the Caribbean; in winter the beach is wild and invigorating. The house set back off the sands, near the trees, offers overnight accom-modation for walkers (for infor-mation tel: 971-176800).

To vary the return, take the COASTAL PATH from Cala Font Salada; this joins your outgoing track and rises back to the Torre d'Aubarca, from where you retrace your steps to **Cala Estreta (3h20min**). I heartily recommend a refreshment stop at the lovely *agroturismo* 2km back up the road — they even offer dusty walkers a free shower!

Top: view across Cala Malsoc (Picnic 31) to the Torre d'Aubarca on its headland; bottom: two solitary tamarind trees mark the approach to beach of Es Verger

Distance/time: 14km/8.7mi; 4h
Grade: easy cliff-top walking after an initial short climb up the low cliff at Cala Pí. Some danger of vertigo where the path nears the edge of the cliff just at the outset.
Equipment: strong walking shoes, water, picnic, suncream, sunhat; swimwear and towel in summer; windproof in winter

How to get there and return: 🚌 or 🚐 (see departure times page 131) to/from Cala Pí
Short walk: Cala Pí — Cala Beltrán — Cala Pí. 4km/2.5mi; 1h. Grade, equipment, access/return as above. Follow the main walk for 30min and return the same way.

This lovely coastal walk allows you to focus on the island's fauna and flora. Seagulls and cormorants, thrushes, rock lizards, perhaps herons and other migratory birds in spring or autumn, and kingfishers have all been spotted in the creek … as well as many interesting varieties of plant life, including wild thyme and rosemary bushes, wild olive, and the occasional tamarind tree. Moreover, the pink sandstone coating the limestone on these cliffs displays wonderfully-interwoven designs where the elements have carved intricate patterns in the rock. This hike makes a complete change from walking in the mountains, and in warmer weather you can swim in one of the pretty coves.

The walk begins at the steps down to the wide creek at **Cala Pí**. Descend to the BEACH, and cross over to walk alongside the BOAT-HOUSES. (After torrential rains this beach can be washed away, in which case you would have to cross the water on planks.) About 50m/yds before the end of the beach, turn up right by the side of the last of the fishermen's houses and walk onto its flat roof, to find the beginning of the ROUGH STEPS UP THE CLIFFS. Once at the top, leave a marker of some sort, as this point of descent is not easily seen on the return. Then turn left to

Lighthouse at Cap Blanc

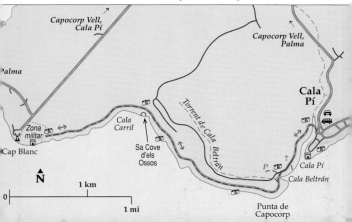

right to follow the rocky cliffs between rock pools, and just make your way along the different levels, enjoying the sea breeze, and watching the cormorants dive for fish. If it is a clear day and visibility is good, the rocky islands of Cabrera are easily seen on the horizon.

When you come to the point where two tamarind trees stand alone by some rock pools, you should climb onto the higher levels to continue.

At **1h20min** you might spot a red arrow painted on a large rock, but do not turn inland as it would suggest — continue along the clifftops, where you will soon find the easily-followed path that rounds the bay of **Cala Carril**. It goes through one or two drystone walls, and in **2h** you reach the MILITARY BOUNDARY FENCE at **Cap Blanc** which blocks access to the watchtower just ahead. The fence is broken, and I suppose many carry on to the tower, but officially this is forbidden.

Leaving Cap Blanc, enjoy different views on the return, among them the huge **Cove d'els Ossos** (the 'Cave of Bones'), and many other smaller ones, at the foot of these impressive cliffs, but please remember to *take extreme care* along this high cliff-edge. You return to **Cala Pí** after **4h**.

follow the cliff path. Soon it descends a little gully, then rises again, before going through a gap in an old stone wall.

Do stop and turn round just beyond the wall, for the best view of beautiful Cala Pí creek, an ideal spot for photography. Then walk on, past scented shrubs, being *extremely careful* where the path skirts the edge of the cliff. Now you have a good view of the watchtower atop the cliff on the opposite side of the cove.

At **20min** keep left just before a group of shady pines, and meet a wide track that rounds the cove of **Cala Beltrán**; end the short walk here, exploring the many crisscross paths around the edge of this wild and pretty creek (Picnic 32). The water in the tiny cove is usually clear and invites you to swim on a calm day, but do not attempt to swim when there is a heavy swell — the force of the waves coming in between the narrow rock walls is tremendous. To continue the main walk, round the cove of Cala Beltrán on the wide track through the trees (there is a short-cut marked by a cairn), and come onto the open cliffs on **Capocorp Point** (**30min**). Turn

TRANSPORT TIMETABLES

Timetables are given on pages 132-133 for all the transport used to get to the walks and picnics in this book. Use the alphabetical list of destinations below to find the appropriate timetable. **Do *not* rely solely on these timetables.** For the most part, we have shown only departures convenient for walkers, not *all* train or bus departures. Get an up-to-date list from the tourist information office when you arrive on the island, or consult the web sites shown on page 7 in advance and download their full timetables. Most timetables shown here operate in

winter, and there may be more frequent departures in summer. ('Summer' timetables are usually valid from 1.5 until 30.9, but this period is flexible — it depends on the weather and how many tourists are about!) If you are staying outside Palma, ask at your hotel about useful local bus services in your area; *there are many more services than those listed here.* See pages 8-9 for town plan of Palma and where to board the appropriate bus. *All departures are daily, unless otherwise coded.*

Destination

Alaró: This is a 🚋 + 🚌 service, Service IB-10 (see http://tib.caib.es) using the Inca train to Consell, then bus to Alaró. Trains and connecting buses approximately half-hourly from Mon-Fri; on Sat/Sun/holidays buses depart Consell at 09.15, 09.50, 10.30, 11.05, 11.45, 16.45, 17.20, 18.00, 18.35, 19.15; depart Alaró at 08.45, 09.40, 10.00, 10.55, 11.15, 16.15, 17.10, 17.30, 18.25, 18.45

Alcúdia: see Timetables 4 and 9*

Andratx: see Timetables 5 and 7

Artà: see Timetable 1

Caimari: see Timetable 3

Cala Pí: This is a summer-only 🚌 service, Service IB-33 (see http://tib.caib.es), with departures Mon-Sat from Palma at 13.00 and 18.30; return from Cala Pí at 19.55

Cala Ratjada: see Timetable 1

Cala Sant Vicenç: see Timetable 9*

Ca'n Picafort: see Timetable 9*

Cúber Lake: see Timetable 9*

Deià: see Timetable 8

Escorca: see Timetable 9*

Inca: see Timetables 3, 4, 6, 10

Lloseta: see Timetable 10

Lluc: see Timetables 3 and 9*

Mirador de Ses Barques: see Timetable 9*

Peguera: see Timetable 5

Pollença: see Timetables 6 and 9*

Port d'Alcúdia: see Timetables 4 and 9*

Port d'Andratx: see Timetable 5

Port de Pollença: see Timetables 6 and 9*

Port de Sóller: see Timetables 8, 9*, 12*, 13*

S'Arracó: see Timetable 7*

Sa Calobra: see Timetables 9* and 13*

Sant Elm: see Timetable 7*

Santa Eugènia: see Timetable 2

Santa Maria: see Timetables 6, 10

Sencelles: see Timetable 2

Sóller: see Timetables 8, 9*, 11, 12*

Son Marroig: see Timetable 8

Valldemossa: see Timetable 8

*indicates services operating outside Palma

1 🚌 IB-26 Palma • Artà • Cala Ratjada

	Mondays to Saturdays				Sundays/holidays	
Palma	10.00	13.30	17.30	19.15	10.00	19.15
Artà	11.30	15.00	19.00	20.45	11.30	20.45
Cala Ratjada	12.00	15.30	19.30	21.15	12.00	21.15
Cala Ratjada	07.45	09.15	14.30	17.10	07.45	17.10
Artà	08.15	09.45	15.00	17.40	08.15	17.40
Palma	09.45	11.15	16.30	19.10	09.45	19.10

NB: There is also an IB-26 🚌 + 🚌 service with two early-morning departures via Manaco station, but it does not operate on Sundays.

2 🚃+🚌 IB-16 Palma • Santa Eugènia • (Sencelles)

For this service take a train from Palma to Santa Maria station (journey time 25min), then connecting bus. *Mon-Fri:* trains depart Palma at 06.50, 07.50, 08.25, 09.25, 10.50, and from 12.25-20.25 hourly; buses depart Santa Maria at 07.35, 08.20, 08.50, 09.50, 11.20 and from 12.50-20.50; journey time to Santa Eugènia 15min. Return buses from Sencelle at 11.55, 18.25, from Santa Eugènia at 12.05 and from 13.35-20.35 hourly. *Sat/Sun holidays:* trains depart Palma at 09.55, 11.45; buses depart Santa Maria at 10.20, 12.20 Return buses from Sencelles at 11.55, 19.25, from Santa Eugènia at 12.05, 19.35.

3 🚃+🚌 IB-36 Palma • Inca • Caimari • Lluc

For this service take a train from Palma to Inca station (journey time 35min), then connecting bus. *Mon-Fri:* trains depart Palma at 07.20, 08.50, 10.25, 11.50, 13.25; buses depart Inc at 08.10, 09.40C, 11.10, 12.40C, 14.10; journey time to Caimari 15min, to Lluc 35min Return buses from Lluc 14.55, 17.55 (via Caimari), also from Caimari at 16.45, 19.45 *Sat/Sun/holidays:* trains depart Palma at 08.00, 11.45; buses depart Inca at 08.45C, 12.30 Return bus from Lluc only at 13.15 (via Caimari), also from Caimari at 19.20.
C: only to Caimari, not to Lluc

4 🚌 IB-21 Palma • Inca • Alcúdia • Port d'Alcúdia

For this service take a bus from Palma. Journey times are Palma to Inca 30min, Inca t Alcúdia 30min, Alcúdia to the Port 15min. *Mon-Sat:* buses depart Palma at 08.00, 09.30 10.15, 11.00, 11.30, 12.00, 13.00, 14.00, 15.00, 16.00, 16.30, 17.00, 18.00, 19.00, 20.00 depart Inca 30min later, depart Alcúdia 1h later. Buses depart Port d'Alcúdia at 06.50, 07.45 08.45, 09.15, 09.45, 10.15, 11.15, 12.15, 13.15, 14.15, 14.45, 15.15, 16.15, 17.15, 18.15 19.15; depart Alcúdia 10min later, depart Inca 40min later, arrive Palma 1h10min later *Sun/holidays:* buses depart Palma at 09.30, 11.00, 13.00, 17.00, 21.00; depart Inca 30mi later, depart Alcúdia 1h later. Buses depart Port d'Alcúdia at 07.50, 09.20, 11.20, 15.20 18.20; depart Alcúdia 10min later, depart Inca 40min later, arrive Palma 1h10min later.

5 🚌 IB-35 Palma • Peguera • Andratx • Port d'Andratx

Frequent departures, too numerous to list. Approximate journey times: Palma — Peguera 55min; Peguera — Andratx: 20min; Andratx — Port: 10min. Buses depart Palma daily a 06.30 and approximately every 45 minutes thereafter until 20.40; another bus departs Palm at 21.00 but terminate at Andratx. Departures from the Port to Palma begin at 06.4 (approximately every 45 minutes). Use this service to connect with buses for Sant Elm and S'Arracó (see Timetable 7 below).

6 🚌 IB-22 Palma • Santa Maria • Inca • Pollença and Por

	Mondays to Fridays					Saturdays			Sun/holidays	
Palma	09.00	11.00	13.30	17.00	19.15	11.00	13.30	18.00	10.00	20.3
S Maria	09.20	11.20	13.50	17.20	19.35	11.20	13.50	18.20	10.20	20.5
Inca	09.30	11.3	14.00	17.00	19.45	11.30	14.00	18.30	10.30	21.1
Pollença	10.00	12.00	14.30	18.00	20.15	12.00	14.30	19.00	11.00	21.3
Port	10.15	12.15	14.45	18.15	20.30	12.15	14.45	91.15	11.15	21.4
Port	07.15	09.15	11.00	14.30	17.00	09.30	11.00	14.00	08.45	18.4
Pollença	07.30	09.30	11.15	14.45	17.15	09.45	11.15	14.15	09.00	19.00
Inca	08.00	10.00	11.45	15.15	17.45	10.15	11.45	14.45	09.30	19.3
S Maria	08.10	10.10	11.55	15.25	17.55	10.25	11.55	14.55	09.40	19.4
Palma	08.30	10.30	12.15	15.45	18.15	10.45	12.15	15.15	10.00	20.00

7 🚌 IB-35 Andratx • Sant Elm ('Line 100' bus, via S'Arracó)

Departs Andratx 08.00, 09.20, 10.40, 14.00, 15.20, 16.40 (journey time 40min)
Departs Sant Elm 08.40, 10.00, 11.20, 14.40, 16.00, 17.20 (journey time 40min)

▄▄ IB-09 Palma • Valldemossa • Deià • Sóller and Port

Departs Palma 07.30*, 08.00+•, 09.30•V, 10.30*+, 10.00•V, 11.30*•V, 13.00•V, 13.30*+, 15.30*, 16.30*V, 17.30•V, 18.30•, 19.30*•. Approximate journey times: Palma — Valldemossa: 30min; Valldemossa — Deià: 15min; Deià — Sóller (Plaça América): 20min; Sóller — Port: 10min

Departs Port Sóller 07.00*, 07.30+, 08.00•, 09.30*+, 11.30•, 13.30*, 15.30*, 17.30*, 18.30*, 19.30+

Departs Sóller (Plaça América) 07.10*, 07.40+, 08.05•, 09.40*+, 11.30•, 13.40*, 15.40*, 17.40*, 18.35•, 19.40+

Departs Deià 07.30*, 08.00+, 08.30•, 10.00*+, 12.00•, 14.00•, 16.00•, 18.00•, 19.00•, 20.00+

Departs Valldemossa 08.00*, 08.30+, 09.00•, 10.30*+, 11.00•, 12.30*•, 13.30•, 14.30*, 15.00+, 15.30*, 16.30*, 17.30*, 18.00•, 18.30*, 19.00*, 19.30•, 20.30+
*Mon-Fri, +only Sat, •only Sun/holidays, V: terminates at Valldemossa

▄▄ IB-15 Ca'n Picafort — Port de Sóller (or Sa Calobra)

summer services (daily except Sundays; winter service may be very restricted)

Departures	Port de Sóller	Lluc/Sa Calobra	Port de Sóller	Departures	Port de Sóller	Lluc/Sa Calobra	Port de Sóller
Ca'n Picafort	09.00	09.00	15.00	Port Sóller	09.00		15.00
Port Alcúdia	09.30	09.30	15.30	Sóller	09.10		15.10
Alcúdia	09.45	09.45	15.45	Ses Barques	09.40		15.40
Port Pollença	10.00	10.00	16.00	Escorca	10.00		16.00
Cala S Vicenç	10.10	10.10	16.10	Lluc	10.20	16.00**	16.20
Pollença	10.20	10.20	16.20	Pollença	11.00	16.35	16.35
Lluc	10.45	10.45*	16.45	Cala S Vicenç	10.55		
Escorca	11.00		17.00	Port Pollença	11.10	16.50	17.00
Ses Barques	11.35		17.35	Alcúdia	11.30	17.00	17.15
Sóller	11.50		17.50	Port Alcúdia	11.35	17.05	17.20
Port Sóller	12.00		18.00	Ca'n Picafort	12.00	17.30	17.45

Stops at Lluc for 1h, then goes on to Sa Calobra, arriving approximately 12.50
* Begins at Sa Calobra, departing 15.00; stops at Lluc for 1h

▄▄ Palma • Santa Maria • Lloseta • Inca*

Departs Palma (Mon-Fri): 05.50, 06.21, 06.50, 07.20, 07.50, 08.25, 08.50; then every hour at 25 and 50 minutes past the hour until 21.25; then 22.00; *departs Palma (Sat, Sun/holidays):* 06.00, 06.45, 07.25, 08.00, 08.40, 09.15, 09.55, 10.30, 11.10, 11.45, 12.25, 13.00, 13.40, 14.15, 14.55, 15.30, 16.10, 16.45, 17.25, 18.00, 18.40, 19.15, 20.30, 21.10, 22.00
Departs Inca (Mon-Fri): 06.34, 06.55, 07.27, 08.00, 08.41, 09.11, 09.41; then every hour at 11 and 41 minutes past the hour until 21.41; then 22.15 and 22.48; *departs Inca (Sat, Sun/holidays):* 07.17, 07.48, 08.32, 09.03, 09.47, 10.18, 11.12, 11.33, 12.17, 12.48, 13.32, 14.03, 14.47, 15.18, 16.02, 16.33, 17.17, 17.48, 18.32, 19.03, 19.47, 20.18, 21.02, 21.34, 22.12, 22.48
Stops at Santa Maria approximately 19min from Palma and at Lloseta 32min from Palma; stops at Lloseta 9min from Inca and at Santa Maria 18min from Inca

▄▄ Palma • Sóller

Departs Palma: 08.00, 10.50, 12.15, 13.30, 15.10, 19.30
Departs Sóller: 08.00, 09.10, 10.50, 12.15, 14.00, 18.30, 19.00•
•Sun only

▄▄ Sóller • Port de Sóller • Sóller

Departs Sóller: 07.00, 08.00, 08.30+, 09.00, 09.30+, 10.00, 10.30, 11.00, 11.25, 12.00, 12.30, 13.00, 13.25, 14.00, 14.30, 15.00, 15.30, 16.00, 16.30, 17.00, 17.30, 18.00, 19.00, 19.30, 20.30
Departs Port: 07.30, 08.25, 09.00+, 09.30, 10.00+, 10.25, 11.00, 11.30, 12.00, 12.30, 13.00, 13.25, 14.00, 14.30, 15.00, 15.30, 16.00, 16.30, 17.00, 17.30, 18.00, 18.30, 19.00, 19.30, 20.00, 20.30
+Sat only

▄▄ Port de Sóller • Sa Calobra

Daily (depending on the weather; in high summer there may be more frequent departures);
see http://tramontanacruceros.com
Departs Port de Sóller: 10.00, 11.00, 12.45, 15.00; *departs Sa Calobra* 12.00, 14.00, 16.45

● Index

Geographical names comprise the only entries in this index; for non-geographical subjects, see Contents, page 3. A page number in *italic type* indicates a map; **bold type** refers to a photograph or drawing. Both of these may be in addition to a text reference on the same page. 'TM' refers to the walking map on the reverse of the touring map. Pronunciation hints follow all place names.

GLOSSARY

(M) Mallorquín; (S) Spanish;

atalaya (S) — *see* talaia

avenc (M) — crater, deep pit

baix (M), *bajo* (S) — low

barranc (M), *barranco* (S) — ravine

*caça a coll (M) — thrush-netting

caçador (M) — hunter

camí (M), *camino* (S) — road, way

ca'n (M) — 'case d'en' ('house of')

canaleta (S) — *see* síquia

carrer (M), *calle* (S) — street

*casa de neu (M), *casa de nieve* (S) — snow pit

coll (M), *collado* (S) — saddle

*coll de caçar (M) — place for thrush-netting (literally, 'hunting at the saddle')

coma (M) — valley floor

comedero (S) — feeding ground

cordillera (S) — mountain range

coto privado de caza (S) — private hunting ground; *see also* vedat

cova, cove (M), *cueva* (S) — cave

dalt (M), *alto* (S) — high

embalse (S) — reservoir

ermita (M, S) — hermitage

estret (M) — narrow pass

finca (S) — farm

*see pages 58-63 for more details

font (M), *fuente* (S) — spring

fronton (M) — pelota court

*forn de calç (M), *horno de cal* (S) — lime oven

mij (M), *medio* (S) — middle

mola (M) — table mountain

morro (M, S) — cliff-top

pas (M) — mountain pass

passeig (M), *paseo* (S) — walk or walkway

penya (M), *pena* (S) — cliff

pla (M), *planicie* (S) — plain

platja (M), *playa* (S) — beach

pou (M), *pozo* (S) — well

puig (M), *pico* (S) — mountain

*santuari (M) — hermitage, monastery

senda (S) — footpath, trail

serra (M), *sierra* (S) — mountain range

*síquia (M), *canaleta* (S) — irrigation channel, watercourse

*sitja (M) — fireplace used in the charcoal industry

son (M) — 'estate of'

*talaia (M), *atalaya* (S) — ancient watchtower

talaiot (M) — prehistoric stone structure

torrent (M), *torrente* (S) — stream (Mallorca has no rivers)